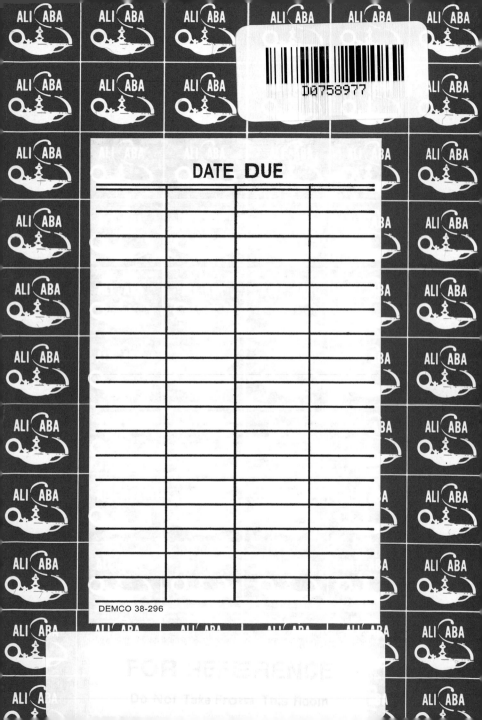

DATE DUE

DEMCO 38-296

PLAIN AND ACCURATE STYLE IN COURT PAPERS

American Law Institute American Bar Association Committee on Continuing Professional Education

As of November 1987

Executive Director: Paul A. Wolkin
Counselor: Michael Greenwald
Administrative Assistant: Donna K. Maropis
. *Assistant:* Mary E. Herzog

OFFICE OF COURSES OF STUDY
Director: Donald M. Maclay
Associate Director: Alexander Hart
Assistant Directors: Nancy A. Kane;
David M. Maola; Kevin J. O'Connor

OFFICE OF BOOKS
Director: Sharon T. Walsh
Associate Director: James D. Maugans
Assistant Directors: Margaret McCarthy;
Carolyn Muldoon
Acquisitions Counselor: Meyer Kramer
Editorial Assistant: Thea R. Clark

OFFICE OF PERIODICALS
Director: Mark T. Carroll
Assistant Directors: Debra DeSantis;
Eileen Kenney; Carla A. Lewis
Editorial Assistant: Linnae Coss

OFFICE OF RESEARCH AND DEVELOPMENT
Director: Mark Mendenhall

OFFICE OF AUDIO AND VIDEO LAW REVIEWS
Director: Susan T. O'Connor
Video Production Manager: Matt Yaple
Administrative Assistant: Linda Brickle

OFFICE OF SPECIAL PROJECTS
Director: George M. Gold

AMERICAN LAW NETWORK
Director: Lawrence F. Meehan, Jr.

AMERICAN INSTITUTE
FOR LAW TRAINING WITHIN THE OFFICE
Director: Richard D. Lee

OFFICE OF ADMINISTRATIVE SERVICES
Director: Walter A. McLaughlin
Administrative Assistant:
Kathleen M. Kilgannon
Chief Accountant: William J. McCormick
Assistant Auditors: Debra Foley;
William P. Thornton
Plant Assistant: Edward Carnes

SPECIAL SERVICES
Meeting Coordinator: Kathleen C. Peters
Production and Design: Robert W. O'Leary
Assistants: Peter J. McGrenaghan;
Doug Smock
Phototypesetters: John Davis;
Rei Murakami
Management Information Systems Director:
Joe Mendicino
Computer Operations: John J. Latch
Assistant: Teri Y. Broadnax
Librarian: Loretta U. McConnell
Librarian: Pearl Li
Professional Relations: J. Stuart Torrey
Marketing Analysis: Kathleen H. Lawner

4025 Chestnut Street, Philadelphia, Pennsylvania 19104

R

PLAIN AND ACCURATE STYLE IN COURT PAPERS

Irwin Alterman
of the Michigan and New York Bars

AMERICAN LAW INSTITUTE-AMERICAN BAR ASSOCIATION
COMMITTEE ON CONTINUING PROFESSIONAL EDUCATION
4025 CHESTNUT STREET • PHILADELPHIA • PENNSYLVANIA 19104

Library of Congress Catalog Number: 87-70733

© 1987 by The American Law Institute. All rights reserved

Second Printing, 1987

Third Printing, 1987

Printed in the United States of America

ISBN: 0-8318-0563-3

James D. Maugans of the ALI-ABA staff
supervised the production of this book

The views and conclusions expressed herein are those of
the author and not necessarily those of the American Law
Institute-American Bar Association Committee on Continuing Professional Education or of its sponsors.

Foreword

In 1979, ALI-ABA published *The Grammatical Lawyer,*
to help lawyers attain, in the words of the author,
Morton S. Freeman, Esquire, "an acceptable standard
of formal English." That book has proven to be one of
ALI-ABA's best sellers.

Plain and Accurate Style in Court Papers seeks to provide, not an acceptable standard of formal English,
but an acceptable standard of style for complaints, answers, motions, discovery matters, and briefs —
documents filed with the clerk of court. The volume
serves in many capacities — as a manual of design, a
system of citations, and a purveyor of simple and accurate language. The directions and examples that it
offers, while useful to lawyers, are even more valuable
to legal secretaries and word-processing personnel.

The original manuscript was written by a member
of the Michigan bar for Michigan lawyers, published
in Volume 2 of the Law Review of the Thomas A.
Cooley Law School in Lansing, Michigan, and distributed to Michigan lawyers by the State Bar of
Michigan and the Michigan State Bar Foundation. At
the suggestion of ALI-ABA and with the kind permis-
sion of the Michigan publisher and distributors, the

author revised the original materials to emphasize papers prepared for the federal courts of the United States, though most of the basic principles are adaptable to filings in state courts.

ALI-ABA is most grateful to Irwin Alterman, Esquire, for this guide to a technical, yet important, aspect of legal practice.

PAUL A. WOLKIN
Executive Director
American Law Institute-
American Bar Association Committee
on Continuing Professional Education

Preface

This book was originally distributed to the more than 23,000 members of the State Bar of Michigan through a grant from that state bar and its foundation, with the *Cooley Law Review* in Lansing, Michigan, participating as the initial publisher. That manual was well received by the Michigan Bar, the media, and plain English experts. This revised edition is essentially the same as the original one.

Plain and Accurate Style in Court Papers has two basic goals. One is writing "plain" English, namely the elimination of unnecessary "legalese" from all lawsuit papers. The other is accurate writing, for example, using the technical words of the involved rule or statute. The basic premise of the manual is that is it just as easy to use good form as bad form, since both are learned; neither is innate.

The manual is an *approach* to style. It is not a form book, in the sense of a complete set of forms. Rather it dissects the style of the various parts of pleadings, motion papers, discovery papers, briefs, and other lawsuit papers. By applying the principles the manual examines, the reader can create personal forms or revise specific forms taken from form books into plain English.

This manual was written not only for the attorney but also for the secretary, the paralegal, and anyone else involved in, or interested in, lawsuit papers.

IRWIN ALTERMAN

Contents

Chapter 4

Complaints 37

Chapter 5

Answers   61

Chapter 6

Motion Practice   75

Chapter 7

Chapter 8

1

Introduction

This manual is a hybrid. It includes forms but is not a form book. It addresses style but is not a style or language treatise. It comments on procedural rules but is not a rules treatise. It discusses plain writing but in a limited context. It is intended as a practical guide to drafting lawsuit papers in plain and accurate language.

One basic philosophy of this manual is that lawsuit papers should be written in plain and readable language. Legal writing should be good writing. If you think legalese is necessary to impress clients, courts, and other attorneys, this manual is not for you.

An important premise of this manual is that it is just as easy to use good form as bad form. Neither is innate. Both are learned. In fact, good form should be easier; it involves fewer words.

Why does form matter? An attorney once told me that he has a volume practice and doesn't have time to worry about form. "As long as I can get by and not get thrown out of court, I am satisfied," he said. He is wrong. Form is the packaging of legal materials. Just as sharp packaging adds to a gift, good form should create a favorable climate for the relief requested in the document. The user of good form will stand out because the overall quality of legal style is so poor.

This manual is intended, in part, to demonstrate how to eliminate archaic "legalese" from all lawsuit papers.

Legalese exists in various forms. One is the stilted phrase, such as "Now comes the plaintiff." Another is redundancy, such as "each and every," "cease and desist," "from and after," "stipulate and agree." Still another is the unnecessary phrase, often in the form of excessive precision. An example is "the *above-named* plaintiff moves . . . ." Why "above-named?" The word "plaintiff" obviously refers to the plaintiff in that action.

Another form of legalese is the archaic word. My favorite is the "here" family — herein, hereby, herewith, heretofore, hereinabove (or below), hereinafter (or before). These words are aptly called "accumulated rubbish" and "junk antiques." MELLINKOFF, LEGAL WRITING: SENSE & NONSENSE 106.

I do not suggest abandonment of all legal words and phrases. Some are technical words of art that identify legal doctrines, such as res judicata, laches, proximate cause. But most are pure old-fashioned legalese. Mellinkoff cogently analyzed the problem:

The main reason why so many people find legal writing unclear is that it wasn't written for them. Most legal writing isn't written for anybody at all. Most legal writing is written to get it written.

Id. at 65.

Complaints about legal gibberish have been heard for centuries. There is a "superstitious veneration" of form "beyond what is just and reasonable." When forms become "insipid, useless, impertinent . . . .they may and must be removed." Sir Matthew Hale, a 17th century Lord Chief Justice of England, quoted in MELLINKOFF, THE LANGUAGE OF THE LAW 194. Jonathan Swift complained, in GULLIVER'S TRAVELS. So did Thomas Jefferson.

Legal style changes slowly. But it does change, just as surely as "party of the first part" has vanished from contracts.

Much of the blame lies with the form books. Most were written decades ago and have not been updated. They lag behind current style in many respects. For example, many sample forms include complaints and affidavits written in the third person: "That he . . . ." Most attorneys today draft affidavits in the first person.

Not only have law schools failed to relieve the gibberish problem, they often perpetuate it. Law reviews, largely written by professors and top students, are dull even to most lawyers. Other writing by professors isn't much better. Many people consider Harvard the country's best law school. In 1982, a committee of distinguished Harvard professors wrote a lengthy report on the future of legal education there. A keystone of the report was support of clinical education. Consider these excerpts:

> Clinical education means, among other things, learning what it truly means to bring doctrinal and theoretical learning, analytical method, communication and persuasion to the actual treatment of complex and refractory problems, in a manner meeting professional standards of craft and care.

* * *

> Clinical instruction is instruction involving (i) activity by the student (ii) in a professional role (iii) under tutorial supervision, designed to yield both (iv) critical self-analysis of performance or response and (v) reflective consideration of more general legal phenomena.

What did they say? I hope clinical education includes writing for the real world.

Good modern style in lawsuit papers emerged with the Appendix of Forms to the Federal Rules of Civil Procedure. Rule 84 states: "The forms contained in the Appendix of Forms are sufficient under the rules and are intended to indicate the simplicity and brevity of statement which the rules contemplate."

Modern style is used by the most prestigious law firms in New York, Washington, and elsewhere. The opinions of the United States Supreme Court are solid examples of good style and organization of legal arguments. Analyze them to improve your briefing style. Yet the official federal forms are sprinkled with "hereby." The United States Supreme Court still sometimes says, "It is ordered, adjudged, and decreed."

It is unrealistic to expect the total elimination of legalese. Every attorney has some favorite phrases he will not lightly abandon. Fine. Some things in this manual are solely for the purist. These materials are an *approach* to style. Accept what you want.

The materials are selective. For many people they will not replace multivolume form books. But the approach is presented, and you can use it to update the style of any form book you use.

These materials should spur your own thinking. You may improve on the suggestions. You may discover that you rarely need to consult a form book.

Bad form does not necessarily affect a litigant's rights adversely. Preparation of lawsuit papers, like all other procedural matters, is governed by what I call the golden rule of procedure. This rule, which everyone knows but often forgets, appears at the beginning of the rules:

[These rules] shall be construed to secure the just, speedy, and inexpensive determination of every action.

FRCP 1.

The federal pleading rule expressly reaffirms the golden rule. FRCP 8(f). The golden rule is again reflected in the harmless error rule. FRCP 61. (The golden rule is often appropriate but unfortunately is rarely cited in briefs and argument. In many procedural matters it is the rule most on point.) The golden rule should provide comfort for experimenting with the style suggestions in this manual. Unfortunately, some may use it to support a "why bother" attitude.

In addition to plain writing, the other basic philosophy of this manual is accurate writing. Do not write about a party's pleading when you mean a motion. Do not omit language required by a rule or statute. Reading the involved rule or statute is more important than using a form book. The text of the rule or statute, not a form, is the basis for legal writing. Accurate writing in this manual also embraces the kind of paper required and the elements required in the paper. Again, this manual is selective. Its goal is to inspire technical accuracy.

These materials focus on the rules governing practice in civil actions in United States district courts. The approach here will be helpful in other courts as well. Although the manual does not consider appellate practice, the chapter on briefs contains many points you can use there.

This manual departs from the Uniform System of Citation, the so-called Harvard blue book, when doing so furthers the plain English theme advanced here. See Section 7.09.

These materials are in large part for the secretary as well as for the attorney. Quite often the secretary drafts papers. Many attorneys would be receptive to improvement in their drafts and style by their secretaries. The attorney who just wanted to "get by" also remarked that it would be great if his secretary were to improve his style. He did not have the time or desire to do it himself.

The manual is arranged to avoid repetition so that points made in one chapter are generally not covered in other chapters, even though they apply there. For example, the discussion of proof of service, found in Chapter 6 under "Motions," where it is sometimes required, applies elsewhere. The use of unsworn declarations instead of notaries is encouraged for many documents, but this appears only under "Verifications" in Chapter 4.

2

General Style Suggestions

§ 2.01 NAMES OF PARTIES

The designations used for the parties and other actors often contain stilted, unnecessary language. Certainly the technical name of a party must appear in captions and in the initial paragraph of the complaint identifying the party. The beginning of other papers also may contain a technical name. Apart from that, a shortened, readable version is preferable.

The goal is to make the text readable and understandable. You need not strive for exact, technical language each time you refer to a party. But be consistent; referring to the party the same way every time helps the reader tremendously.

The basic ways to refer to parties are (1) the name or abbreviations of the name, (2) functional names, or

(3) as plaintiff and defendant. Let's review some examples in drafting complaints.

First, consider a simple lawsuit involving one plaintiff and one defendant who are natural persons. There is nothing wrong with referring to the parties in the body of the complaint as "plaintiff" and "defendant." You may also refer to them by their names, such as "Smith" and "Jones." After the formal identification, however, you should *not* use such phrases as "defendant Jones" or "Jones, defendant herein," or "the above-named defendant." These are redundant and stilted. The caption makes it clear, and the initial identification in the complaint confirms, that there is a plaintiff named Smith and a defendant named Jones. It should be obvious that "plaintiff" means Smith and "Smith" means plaintiff. Use one designation or the other, but not both.

An action involving more than one natural person with the same last name requires the use of first names, of course. In some instances it may also be appropriate to use descriptive terms. For example, consider a family involved in an automobile accident in which each person sues for injuries. You could refer to the plaintiffs as "plaintiff husband," "plaintiff wife," and "plaintiff daughter."

But basically, when there are multiple plaintiffs or defendants, it is better to abandon the designation "plaintiff" or "defendant" when referring to one member of that group and to use other designations. The names of corporations can readily be abbreviated by eliminating the words "company," "corporation," or "incorporated" or their abbreviations. For example, General Motors Corporation can be shortened to "General Motors." Acronyms are proper but should generally be limited to instances in which the acronym is well known. For example, "ATT" for American Telephone & Telegraph Company. In comparison, Parke-Davis Company should not be abbreviated to "PD." Abbreviations may be limited to the key word or words in a corporate name. For example, Great Scott Super Markets, Inc. may be abbreviated to "Great Scott." Similar rules apply to partnerships and assumed names.

Functional names provide an alternative means of designation that, in many instances, neatly contributes to clarity. Perhaps the easiest example is a group of plaintiffs or defendants with a common characteristic. For example, if the defendants are a partnership and each of the general partners is named individually, instead of listing each partner throughout the complaint, you can simply say "general partners." If the defendants are a number of persons who own real property as tenants in common, you could simply call them collectively "owners."

The use of such descriptive names is particularly appropriate when the legal relationships depend on the status of the parties. For example, in an action between a landlord and a tenant, you could simply refer to the parties as "landlord" and "tenant." Similarly, in a product liability action, you could refer to the defendants as "retailer," "wholesaler," "manufacturer," and "component manufacturer." The possibilities are endless. These functional names add greater clarity because the party's function is more important to understanding the claim than the party's technical name.

Functional names are also desirable when the technical name is lengthy and abbreviation is difficult. For example, labor unions generally have long names. Simply say "union." Government agencies sometimes have long names also. Simply say "agency."

Generally the designation of a party in the complaint will be set forth as part of the paragraph identifying the party.

Example:

Owen Simon ("buyer") resides at . . . .

Do not say:

Owen Simon (hereinafter referred to as the "buyer") resides at . . . .

Because it is obvious that the designation in quotation marks and parentheses ("buyer") means "hereinafter referred to as," this phrase is unnecessary.

Sometimes a group of parties will be referred to by one designation. For example, suppose Simon, Jones, and Smith are joint owners. At the end of the identification of the last member of the group, say "(Simon, Smith, and Jones are collectively the 'owners')."

When an abbreviation is obvious in the context, it need not be inserted in the identification paragraph.

The prior examples involving General Motors, ATT, and Great Scott are typical of this category.

Introductory clauses of all papers should just say "plaintiffs" or "defendants" if the paper is on behalf of all of them, or another short designation if on behalf of less than all.

Examples:

Plaintiffs move . . . .

Defendant Simon objects to the following interrogatories . . . .

If the paper is on behalf of a large number of parties, but not all of those on the same side, simplicity sometimes prompts a less formal approach, such as "Defendant general partners." A preanswer motion or answer should always specifically describe the involved parties. Sometimes it is easier and shorter to identify those not included.

Example:

All defendants except defendants Simon and Rose move . . . .

The body of all other papers should follow the readable style suggested for complaints.

§ 2.02 IDENTIFICATION OF THINGS

Complaints and other lawsuit papers deal not only with parties but also with events, contracts, property, and so forth. Descriptions of these things often contain unnecessary and stilted language. For example, in a complaint seeking specific performance of a contract for the sale of real property, after identifying the contract or offer to purchase, later references to that document can simply be the "offer to purchase" or the "contract." It is unnecessary to say the "above-identified" contract, the contract "herein" or the "said" contract. It is obvious the complaint relates to only one contract. Similarly, after describing the property, simply refer to the "property." No further language is necessary, since only one property is involved in the action.

When the matter is potentially complicated, such as one involving a series of agreements, it is especially appropriate to use short designations that aid the reader. For example, a document might be "1968 amendment." When the context suggests possible confusion, indicate the abbreviation you will use with parentheses and quotation marks, similar to abbreviations of parties, right after the initial identification of the document, event, property, and so forth.

It is important to remember what is or is not necessary to adjudicate your claim. For example, I once drafted a complaint involving property developed under a HUD program. A HUD specialist is very concerned about the differences among the various programs, such as 236, 221(d)(3), and 221(d)(4). A federal or state trial judge of general jurisdiction has neither the time nor the desire to appreciate the subtle differences. After initially explaining the essence of what was involved in the action, I abbreviated it thereafter as the "HUD program." Nothing else was necessary for the purpose of that action.

§ 2.03 NUMBERS

Whatever the rules may be that govern numbers and dollar amounts in real estate and loan transactions, the rules in lawsuits are very simple. First, do not write a number out in words. Simple Arabic numbers suffice. Second, it is ridiculous to list zero cents when the number is rounded off to an even dollar. For example, a contract or injury in the amount of $100,000 should not be written "$100,000.00." The presumption is that such numbers are round numbers. It is highly unlikely that someone would have a contract or an injury of $100,000.12. If an odd number of cents is involved, it should be set forth. Otherwise, omit the ".00."

§ 2.04 CAPITALIZATION

This section reviews "initial caps" — using a capital letter for the first letter of a word. The typeface section will deal with capital letters for the entire word.

Excessive use of capital letters makes reading more difficult and looks unappealing. Generally, capitalize only words that are capitalized in nonlegal writing, such as proper names. Many lawyers capitalize too much. Consider this sentence: "The Plaintiff and the Defendant entered into the Contract . . . ." When I ask lawyers why they use capital letters here, the typical response is that the sentence is about a *particular* plaintiff, a *particular* defendant, and a *particular* contract. These are not abstract words, they say.

That's nonsense. Most nouns of this sort are used to refer to a specific person or thing. Suppose the sample sentence ended with "at plaintiff's office." Would you capitalize "office," since it refers to a specific place? Of course not. Do not capitalize the other words either. A useful guide is When in doubt, do not capitalize.

Many specific rules govern words that frequently appear in lawsuit papers. Here are some examples. One word often used is "court." Do not capitalize the word "court" standing alone. A purist will capitalize when referring to the United States Supreme Court. *See* A UNIFORM SYSTEM OF CITATION § 8 (14th ed). Capitalize the name of a court when stating the full name. You may also capitalize a partial name that includes a word that must otherwise be capitalized. I prefer not to capitalize a reference to a federal court, such as "sixth circuit," because it is not the full court name, although others disagree. Do not capitalize the word "judge" or "justice" unless the person's name follows. A purist will capitalize if it is a supreme court Justice. However, capitalize titles when they refer to one specific person, such as President or Attorney General.

These guidelines cover references to lawsuit papers. Do not capitalize a reference to a pleading or other paper with a one word or short title, such as the "complaint," "stipulation," "order," or "proof of service," except as part of the caption in that document itself.

You may capitalize the full title of lawsuit papers of several words, such as "Brief in Support of Motion for Preliminary Injunction." Except for the caption of that document itself, try to shorten these cumbersome titles, such as "preliminary injunction brief." Do not generally capitalize "affidavit," but do so if you include the affiant's name, for example, Affidavit of Owen Simon. Use initial caps for "Exhibit" because it is usually followed by a capital letter or number.

The official name of federal statutes is generally written with initial capital letters. The statutes themselves frequently state the official name this way. For example, the codification of one statute states: "This Chapter may be cited as the 'Securities Exchange Act of 1934.'" 15 USC 78a. *See also* 15 USC 77a ("Securities Act of 1933"). Frequently, the official name is just set forth in the public act. For example, "This Act may be cited as the 'Civil Service Reform Act of 1978.'" P.L. 95-454, § 1, 5 USCA 1101 note; "This title may be cited as the 'Monetary Control Act of 1980.'" P.L. 96-221, § 1, 12 USCA 226 note.

§ 2.05   TYPEFACE

Just as you should avoid unnecessary initial caps, you should also avoid writing individual words in all capital letters Do not say "PLAINTIFF" or the "CON-TRACT."

Headings or subheadings are preferably in initial caps or, alternatively, in lower case, under the same rules as words in a sentence. Avoid all-caps. When the letters in a phrase or sentence are all the same size, the words are harder to read. Studies have confirmed this. Use all-caps, if you wish, for portions of the caption or for major neutral headings in briefs, pleadings, and other papers. But use initial caps or no caps on the key headings you really want the reader to read.

If you use an all-cap typeface for certain words or kinds of headings, be consistent in that paper and other related papers.

§ 2.06 DOCUMENT DESIGN

The concept of document design in legal papers surfaced as part of the current plain English movement. If it sounds suspiciously like a public relations firm marketing tool, don't worry. You *are* marketing your lawsuit. You want to persuade the reader. Plain English words in a poor format will only go part of the way.

Design includes many things. Capitalization and typeface are part of design. But there are other elements. One is making citations unobtrusive, not the most dominant feature. Another is organization and subheadings. These are reviewed elsewhere.

A document should *look* readable. Use short paragraphs. Headings and subheadings should extend only part way across a page so they stand out.

Example

Do not use:

Simon cannot demonstrate a likelihood of success on the merits

Instead, use:

Simon cannot demonstrate
a likelihood of success
on the merits

A lengthy laundry list should preferably be postured so that it turns out to be 1-2-3 rather than a-b-c. A document on 11-inch paper, now required in federal court, looks less ominous. Use that size for briefs in state courts if permitted.

Staple only in the upper left corner, at the angle in which a page is normally turned. Staples across the entire top make it harder to turn pages.

Provide a table of contents in long trial court briefs. Readers appreciate this help. (Some people believe a table should be more than just "design"; it should be part of the persuasion process.)

3

Captions

§ 3.01 NAME OF COURT

The designation of the court belongs at the top of the first page of a lawsuit paper. The proper style in federal court is

UNITED STATES DISTRICT COURT
[FOR THE] EASTERN DISTRICT OF
MICHIGAN
SOUTHERN DIVISION

You may omit the words in brackets. When the district has divisions, you must include this information. *See* FRCP, Appendix of Forms, Introductory Statement.

The following series is an example of how you can improve your style, one step at a time, in captions for other courts.

Better form:

STATE OF MICHIGAN
IN THE CIRCUIT COURT FOR THE
COUNTY OF WAYNE

Even better:

STATE OF MICHIGAN
IN THE CIRCUIT COURT FOR
WAYNE COUNTY

Best form:

STATE OF MICHIGAN
CIRCUIT COURT FOR WAYNE COUNTY

STATE OF MICHIGAN
WAYNE COUNTY CIRCUIT COURT

§ 3.02 NAMES OF PARTIES IN SUMMONS AND COMPLAINT

The summons and complaint must set forth the accurate, technical name of every party. FRCP 4(b), 10(a). In every action of real significance, you should always check to be certain you know the technical name of a corporation or partnership, particularly those formed in your state. It can be very embarrassing with an important client not to have the exact name. For example, early in my career I prepared a complaint for Texaco, designating the company in the caption and elsewhere as "Texaco, Inc." I later discovered the company did not use a comma in its name.

The technical name of a party is the name on file with the appropriate government agency or official, in exactly the form in which it is on file. Like Texaco, some entities do not use commas. A corporation has the option of ending its corporate name with incorporated, corporation, company, or the usual abbreviations of these words. Check the designation used in the articles of incorporation.

Be aware that a client may sometimes mislead you with respect to its own name. For example, for many years the letterhead of a Detroit supermarket chain read: "Great Scott! Supermarkets, Inc." However, its technical name did not include the exclamation point, and the word "supermarkets" was split into two words. Just as with legal style in general, attention to details, such as the proper corporate name, will be rewarding in the long run.

§ 3.03 DESIGNATION OF PARTIES IN OTHER PAPERS

The federal rules expressly permit all papers other than the summons and complaint to list only the first plaintiff and first defendant followed by "et al." FRCP 10(a), 7(b)(2). Frequently a lawyer's secretary will type the entire list of parties on each paper. This is unnecessary, regardless of the kind of action or the nature of the paper.

On a very few occasions it may be desirable to list all of the parties. For example, this might serve a purpose on an injunction or final judgment. Otherwise, it is unnecessary, even if the party you represent and file papers for does not end up being listed in the short caption.

Because of the short caption rule, attorneys frequently pay careful attention to which party they designate first as the plaintiff or defendant in the complaint. That will be the name of the action for all time. Absent any special reason, list first the parties most central to the lawsuit.

Sometimes the case name is fortuitous. Many school children joined in the complaint that resulted in the United States Supreme Court's 1954 desegregation decision. The names were listed alphabetically; therefore, the case will always be known as *Brown v Board of Education.*

§ 3.04 OTHER REQUIRED INFORMATION

The caption must, of course, include the civil action number. FRCP 10(a). I prefer "Civil No" preceding the number. Some use "No" or "Case No." Some federal courts require the name of the judge assigned to the case to be included, either above or below the case number. Some require the names and addresses of the attorneys. The caption must also include the type of document (for example, answer, motion). *Id.*

§ 3.05 THE NATURE OF AN ENTITY

The popular convention in captions is to list after each entity that it is a "Delaware corporation," or "limited partnership," or an "unincorporated association," or some other appropriate designation. Although this convention is not expressly required by the rules and is generally unnecessary, it is harmless. The federal rules state that it is not necessary to list the capacity of a party in the complaint except to the extent required to show the court's jurisdiction. FRCP 9(a). Normally a description of the nature of the entity will appear in the first portion of the body of the complaint.

§ 3.06 INDIVIDUAL USING ASSUMED NAME

The name of a business is often an assumed name adopted by an individual who never formed an entity. In that case he operates the business individually. Presumably, he filed an assumed name certificate for the business name. The action may be brought by or against the individual who is the real party in interest. FRCP 17(a). *See also* FRCP 17(b). It is always safe to name the individual followed by "d/b/a" (doing business as).

Examples:

OWEN SIMON,

　　　　Plaintiff [or defendant]

———————————

OWEN SIMON d/b/a OWEN'S LEGAL WRITING SCHOOL,
Plaintiff [or defendant]

§ 3.07 CLASS ACTIONS

The usual designation of a class action in the caption of the complaint is

OWEN SIMON, on behalf of himself and all others similarly situated,
Plaintiffs,

-v-

ABC CORP.,
Defendant

Generally, attorneys use this complete designation in later papers unless, of course, the court has ordered that the action may not proceed as a class action.

§ 3.08 GOVERNMENT OFFICIALS

A government official sued in his official capacity may be designated by his title rather than his name. FRCP 25(d)(2). The court may require you to add the person's name. *Id.* You may initially designate the person by name, usually followed by the title.

Examples:

OWEN SIMON, Attorney General
or
ATTORNEY GENERAL

When the caption includes the individual's name, automatically change the caption to the name of a successor. FRCP 25(d)(1).

§ 3.09 INFANTS AND INCOMPETENTS

The representative of an infant or incompetent person is the proper party. FRCP 17(c).

Example:

SUSAN ROSE, as guardian
ad litem for Owen Simon,

    Plaintiff,

-v-

ABC CORP.,

    Defendant.

When the named party becomes incompetent during the action, a representative should be substituted as the named party. The federal rules require this to be done by motion. FRCP 25(b).

§ 3.10 REPRESENTATIVE CAPACITY

The real party in interest must be the named party. Persons suing in certain representative capacities may sue and be sued in their own name. FRCP 17(a). It is proper, as with infants and incompetents, that any representative give notice of this status in the caption.

Example:

> OWEN SIMON, as executor of the estate of Susan Rose,
>
> > Plaintiff,

§ 3.11 USE OF *IN RE*

This kind of caption is used in a variety of situations in which there is no "defendant." Many of these are what some courts call miscellaneous matters, as distinguished from lawsuits. A proceeding to quash a grand jury subpoena is often styled something like "*In re* grand jury proceedings." A petition by an attorney to practice before the court or to review a suspension from practice may be, for example, "*In re* Simon." This caption is extensively used in specialized areas, such as bankruptcy, probate, adoption, and similar status situations. It is common in administrative matters, such as licensing and ratemaking. This kind of caption may also be established by the court to designate many actions consolidated or combined for certain purposes. For example, "*In re* Air Crash Disaster at John F. Kennedy Int'l Airport on June 24, 1975."

§ 3.12 CONSOLIDATED ACTIONS

Two different styles are appropriate for the captions of consolidated actions. It is proper to list the parties, in the short form, for the first action with the lower number and then to designate the number of that action along with the numbers of all the consolidated actions.

Example:

> OWEN SIMON,
>> Plaintiff,
>
> -v-   Civil Nos
>   7314, 7415
>
> ABC CORP.,
>> Defendant

This is acceptable even though none of the parties are identical in the consolidated actions.

Another appropriate form, usually used when only two actions are consolidated, is to list the title and number of the other action.

Example:

> OWEN SIMON,
>> Plaintiff,
>
> -v-   Civil No 7314
>
> ABC CORP.,
>> Defendant

> CHARLES WOLFE,
>> Plaintiff,
>
> -v-   Civil No 7415
>
> ABC CORP.,
>> Defendant.

§ 3.13 COUNTERCLAIMS AND CROSS-CLAIMS

Do not designate in the caption any reference to counterclaims and cross-claims. For example, do not say "Defendant and Counterplaintiff." Say "Defendant" only.

§ 3.14 THIRD-PARTY ACTIONS

The title of a third-party action is normally listed in the caption just below the title of the main action. Here is an example in which one of several defendants has filed a third-party complaint:

OWEN SIMON,

    Plaintiff,

-v-

ABC CORP, et al,

    Defendants.

-and-

DEBORAH CHARLES,

    Defendant and

    Third-Party Plaintiff

-v-

XYZ CORP.,

    Third-Party Defendant.

§ 3.15 INTERVENORS

It is not necessary to list the names of intervenors in captions. This is an application of the short caption rule described in Section 3.03.

§ 3.16 PARTY NOT PROPERLY DESIGNATED

Suppose the complaint names as a defendant XYZ, Inc, and XYZ is not a corporation but a division of ABC, Inc. If XYZ is not the lead defendant and will not appear in the short "et al." caption, you obviously do not have to worry about the caption. If XYZ is the lead defendant, then you should use the correct name in your response. In either case, the introductory language of your response should be

> ABC, Inc answers [or, e.g., moves to dismiss] the complaint for the defendant designated as XYZ Inc.

Designating the correct party improperly is different from suing the wrong party. For example, naming a property management company when plaintiff intended the landlord or naming a sales company when plaintiff intended the manufacturer. The defendant in these instances should respond for the entity erroneously named.

§ 3.17 CHANGED CIRCUMSTANCES

Suppose that a party changes names or that the lead plaintiff or defendant (the first one listed) is no longer a party or that an amended complaint changes lead parties or that the lowest number of consolidated cases is over or that other similar changes occur. You should correct the caption in each of these situations to conform to current facts. It is often a difficult task to change court records after the original name has been placed on the computer and docket sheets. The parties may have to live with the original name in court notices. When a party transfers its interest, however, the action is continued with the original party unless the court otherwise directs. FRCP 25(c). Substitution of proper parties after death must be done by court order. FRCP 25(a). You should always substitute the name of a successor public official for the named official if he is sued in his official capacity. FRCP 25(d)(1).

§ 3.18 DOCUMENT TITLE

The designation of the document is part of the "caption." *See* FRCP 10(a), 7(b)(2). Every document filed must have a title even if it is simply "answer," "affidavit," "notice of hearing," "stipulation," or "notice of deposition." The following are the proper titles for the major documents discussed in this manual.

§ 3.18(a) Complaint

The federal rules provide that an action is commenced by filing a "complaint." FRCP 3. The title should simply be "Complaint." The rules do not require any additional description, such as "Verified Complaint," "Complaint For Injunctive Relief," and so on. FRCP 10(a). These adjectives or descriptive phrases are harmless, however, and may be used.

Certain categories of complaints are often called "petitions." Usually a petition involves an action in which the relief sought is a court order in the nature of a historic writ, such as "petition for writ of habeas corpus," or "petition for civil contempt." Unless a petition is filed in an existing action (in which it functions as a motion), the petition is equivalent to a complaint.

§ 3.18(b) Answer

The title is simply "Answer." When the answer includes another pleading, identify it. For example, "Answer and Counterclaim," "Answer and Cross-Claim." Do not include the phrase "affirmative defenses" as part of the title. Listing the party is optional; many attorneys do not. For example, Answer of [Defendant] Owen Simon. You should never add the word "defendant" because every answer is that of a defendant. (A plaintiff's response to a counterclaim is a "reply.")

§ 3.18(c) Motion Practice

There are three levels of specificity in motion practice documents. Some documents have only the generic name:

Notice of Hearing
Proof of Service

Others have some further identification:

Motion for Summary Judgment
Affidavit of Owen Simon
Order of Dismissal as to Defendant Simon

A motion title frequently does not list the party filing it. In an action involving many parties, generally list the party filing the motion if it is filed for fewer than all parties on one side. An affidavit may be simply "Affidavit," because the beginning of the body and the date will identify it for later reference. The better practice, however, is to list the affiant in the title. An order can simply be an "Order." Federal judges often prepare orders that way. Final orders, however, should always be labeled, for example, "Order of Dismissal," so that the clerk will be alerted to close the file. Some judges prefer a specific description on all orders, which the clerk can enter on the docket sheet.

The most detailed and stilted titles occur in briefs in which the parties are often identified.

Examples:

> Plaintiff's Brief in Support of Motion
> for a Preliminary Injunction
>
> Brief in Opposition to Plaintiff's Motion
> for a Preliminary Injunction

Some day a brave lawyer will shorten that cumbersome style. It would be a breakthrough. I do it for reply and supplemental briefs.

Example:

> Reply Brief on the
> Preliminary Injunction Motion

Briefs on appeal are not encumbered with long titles.

§ 3.18(d) Discovery

Deposition notices use a generic title, but other documents often identify the party making the request. When the request is directed to one of several opposing parties, that information is often added.

Examples:

> Notice of Depositions
> Adjourned Notice of Depositions
> Plaintiff's Interrogatories
> Plaintiff's Interrogatories to Defendant Simon, First
> Set
> Answers to Plaintiff's Interrogatories

The "First Set" is frequently part of the psychology of signaling the opponent that this will be a hard-fought case, even if every conceivable question is in the first set.

4

Complaints

§ 4.01 INTRODUCTORY CLAUSES

The old-fashioned preamble for complaints, still recommended in various form books, goes something like this:

> NOW COMES the above named Owen Simon, plaintiff herein, by and through Darrow & Williams, his attorneys of record, and shows unto this Honorable Court as follows:

Some form books suggest a remarkably simple alternative:

> The plaintiff says:

Although the suggested short form certainly follows the theme of these materials, I prefer a middle ground that serves to keep the law firm name in the forefront.

Example:

> Plaintiff Owen Simon, by his attorneys Darrow & Williams, for his complaint states:

If there are multiple plaintiffs, you may omit their names and simply say "Plaintiffs, by their attorneys . . . ."

§ 4.02 OUTLINE OF COMPLAINT

The outline of all complaints is subject to rules that, of necessity, are somewhat general because of the variety of legal claims and factual complexity.

The federal rules require (1) a short statement showing the court's jurisdiction, (2) "a short and plain statement of the claim showing that the pleader is entitled to relief," and (3) a demand for judgment. FRCP 8(a).

In federal courts, pleading averments must be "simple, concise, and direct." FRCP 8(e)(1). A party may allege facts in the alternative and plead inconsistent claims (or defenses). FRCP 8(e)(2).

A federal complaint starts with the official jurisdictional statement, see FRCP official forms, generally followed with identification of the parties.

In lengthy, complex complaints, it may be helpful to have a paragraph describing the nature of the action ahead of the identification of the parties.

Example:

This is an action seeking a declaratory judgment that a rule of the ABC agency is unconstitutional. The rule provides . . . .

In federal question actions this introductory statement can readily be incorporated in the required jurisdictional averment.

The heart of the claim is set forth in logical progression. First, describe plaintiff's right or defendant's duty, then the invasion or breach, and finally the damage or threatened damage. A good example is an action founded on a written instrument. Identify the instrument, point out the pertinent language or provisions, describe what did or did not happen, and then summarize with what it means in money damages or other relief.

Other actions may require a different approach. In personal injury actions, for example, the duty of care arises in connection with the specific factual situation. First, set forth the events, then the duty in those circumstances, the breach, and the damage.

Considerable background information is often required before reaching the guts of the claim. An example may be a claim dependent on a course of dealing.

The complaint should address all elements necessary for relief. This requires a knowledge of the substantive law. An example is common law fraud, in which you should have averments showing: (1) a material representation (2) that was false, (3) that the defendant knew was false, (4) that the plaintiff relied on (5) to his damage.

A complaint that does not directly address each element is not necessarily dismissed.

. . . the complaint, and other relief-claiming pleadings need not state with precision all elements that give rise to a legal basis for recovery as long as fair notice of the nature of the action is provided. However, the complaint must contain either direct allegations on every material point necessary to sustain a recovery on any legal theory, even though it may not be the theory suggested or intended by the pleader, or contain allegations from which an inference fairly may be drawn that evidence on these material points will be introduced at trial.

5 WRIGHT AND MILLER, FEDERAL PRACTICE AND PROCEDURE §1216 at 120-123.

The court rules expressly require certain kinds of claims to be pleaded with particularity. FRCP 9. Examples are fraud and special damage. The rules also expressly eliminate certain pleading requirements, such as pleading capacity. *Id.*

Following the first claim, you should set out all other alternative or supplemental theories of relief.

Finally, the complaint ends with the prayer or demand for judgment or relief and signature.

§ 4.03 HEADINGS AND MULTIPLE COUNTS

The federal rules require each separate claim for relief to be stated in a separate count "whenever a separation facilitates the clear presentation of the matters set forth." FRCP 10(b).

Counts are usually designated by Roman numerals, such as "Count I." It is not necessary to put the theory in the heading, such as "Implied Contract," though it is not wrong to do so. The problem with stating the theory is that you are usually stuck with it should you subsequently change your approach and later want to claim that the averments really addressed a different theory.

Many attorneys always separate each count. This is safer. But don't be afraid to go the other way in relatively simple actions.

In the federal courts you need not have separate counts when the various theories largely depend on the same facts and require the same relief. An example is a complaint seeking recovery on an express oral contract, implied contract, and unjust enrichment. The last two theories require few additional averments and should not have to be separated unless the factual setting is complex or different for each theory. The official federal forms set the tone by permitting statutory copyright infringement and common law unfair competition in a single count. FRCP Form 17.

Many situations require separation of counts as a practical matter, for example, when not all plaintiffs or not all defendants are involved in each count or when there are different transactions or occurrences.

In which order should the claims appear? Usually the claims should start with the most encompassing and move toward the narrowest and most specific. The most general claim will normally involve the most facts, parties, and damage. Putting it first facilitates presenting all claims, even if the general claim is not the claim with the best chance of winning.

There are two basic styles for designating counts. The traditional one is to place "Count I" after the introductory clause, followed by all relevant averments. "Count II" follows with an incorporation of all prior paragraph numbers relevant to that claim and then the new averments for Count II. The procedure is similar for remaining claims.

An emerging alternative style, which I consider preferable, uses a heading titled "General Allegations" after the introductory clause. This includes all allegations that relate to all or most of the claims. The heading for "Count I" then begins with averments unique to that claim. Each other count similarly sets forth only the averments unique to that count. You may have an incorporation paragraph at the beginning of each count for the "General Allegations." But since the first section is called "General Allegations," I regard such an incorporation as unnecessary.

Apart from headings for counts, a complaint may have a separate series of headings similar to the elements of the claim. This is especially important in complex complaints, but it may also be used effectively in relatively short ones. If the complaint has centered headings for designating counts, these headings for the elements would be placed at the left margin. Otherwise, they belong in the center. When the element headings are the only ones, they may also, at your option, have Roman numeral designations.

One example is the standard form of antitrust price-fixing complaint used by the Department of Justice. The headings, with a minor adjustment required for private actions, are

   I. Jurisdiction
  II. Parties
 III. Co-Conspirators
 IV. Trade and Commerce
  V. Violation Alleged
 VI. Effects
VII. Damage

§ 4.04 PARAGRAPH NUMBERING

The rules require numbered paragraphs, which shall be "limited as far as practicable to a statement of a single set of circumstances." FRCP 10(b). Numerals should be Arabic.

Multiple-count complaints may be numbered in at least three ways. The preferable way is to continue consecutive numbers throughout. For example, assume the first count has 10 paragraphs and the second count incorporates 1 through 7. The preferred form is to adopt 1-7 in paragraph 11:

COUNT II

11. Plaintiff adopts by reference paragraphs 1-7.
12. . . . .

An alternative style, which unnecessarily increases the numbering, is to adopt 1-7 in paragraphs 11-17:

COUNT II

11.-17. Plaintiff adopts by reference paragraphs 1-7.

18. . . . .

Finally, a third style uses paragraphs 1-7 again:

COUNT II

1.-7. Plaintiff adopts by reference paragraphs 1-7 of Count 1.

8. . . . .

Ultimately, this third style will be confusing, because future references to paragraphs would also have to identify the count, particularly for paragraph numbers starting with 8.

Short paragraphs are desirable. Defendants often look for one minor disputed issue to arguably justify denying an entire paragraph (even though this may be contrary to the rules). Short paragraphs that separate potentially multiple averments reduce the use of this ploy.

§ 4.05 JURISDICTIONAL STATEMENT

The official federal forms give suggested language for the allegation of jurisdiction in federal courts. FRCP Form 2. Use them. No reason exists for anything other than minor variations.

The suggested official form language for jurisdiction founded on diversity of citizenship, for example, as applied to a Michigan plaintiff, is this:

Plaintiff is a Michigan corporation having its principal place of business in Michigan, and defendant is a corporation incorporated under the laws of _____ _____ having its principal place of business in a state other than Michigan. The matter in controversy exceeds, exclusive of interest and costs, the sum of $10,000.

The language may sound somewhat redundant, but it is required in the statute conferring jurisdiction. 28 USC 1332. Note — the official form says "Ten Thousand Dollars." These materials suggest the use of Arabic numerals only. The official form also says "the State of" before a state's name. These words are superfluous.

For federal question jurisdiction, the appropriate language, with slight variations under the guidelines of these materials, is, for example:

The action arises under the federal securities laws [or alternatively state the specific law, such as "Section 10(b) of the Securities Exchange Act of 1934"], more particularly 15 USC 78j(b), as more fully appears below.

Under the general federal question jurisdiction, it used to be necessary to also allege that the matter in controversy exceeded $10,000. This jurisdictional requirement was removed by 1976 and 1980 amendments. Even before the amendments, many claims arose under statutes regulating commerce under which there is no jurisdictional minimum amount requirement. 28 USC 1337.

You should also recite (and track the language from) any statute conferring jurisdiction or creating a private right of action apart from the judicial code, that is Title 28 of the United States Code. For example, antitrust complaints usually contain the following:

> The subject matter jurisdiction of this court arises under 28 USC 1337 in that this is (a) an action under Section 4 of the Clayton Act, 15 USC 15, to recover threefold the damages sustained by plaintiffs and all others similarly situated, and the cost of suit, including reasonable attorney fees, for injuries sustained by plaintiffs and all others similarly situated in their business and/or property by reason of defendants' violation of Section 1 of the Sherman Act, 15 USC 1, and (b) an action under Section 16 of the Clayton Act, 15 USC 26, for injunctive relief for threatened loss or damage to plaintiffs and all others similarly situated by defendants' violation of Section 1 of the Sherman Act, 15 USC 1.

§ 4.06 IDENTIFICATION OF PARTIES

Generally each party is identified in a separately numbered paragraph. There are no court rules governing the elements required in identification; rather they are a matter of custom.

Identification of a natural person usually consists of merely listing the person's residence or business. Many people do not want to disclose their residence address; therefore, many attorneys limit themselves to a business address or a city or even omit the address altogether. If a party is a public official whose involvement in the action is in his official capacity, it is sufficient to merely identify the person by title. Similarly, if an individual party is connected with an entity that is also a party, it is sufficient to identify that person by title.

Examples:

2. Plaintiff Owen Simon resides at 221 English Rd, Detroit, Michigan.

2. Plaintiff Owen Simon has a place of business in Southfield, Michigan

2. Defendant James Blanchard is the Governor of Michigan.

2. Defendant Owen Simon is the branch manager of ABC Corp.

Identification of corporations normally consists of the state of incorporation and the address of an office. The cumbersome traditional form of identification is

Plaintiff ABC Company is a corporation incorporated under, and by virtue of, the laws of the State of Michigan, having a principal place of business at 2200 Woodward Avenue, Detroit, Michigan.

A concise and appropriate version would be

ABC Company is a Michigan corporation with an office at 2200 Woodward Avenue, Detroit, Michigan.

Partnerships are generally identified by the state of formation and by whether they are general or limited. For example:

2. Writing Style Associates is a Michigan limited partnership with an office at 2200 Woodward Avenue, Detroit, Michigan.

It is not necessary to specifically list the act under which the partnership was formed or any information relating to the filing of a partnership certificate.

Unincorporated associations are generally identified by indicating that the party is an unincorporated association, along with the address.

§ 4.07 CLASS ACTION

Class action averments are generally placed after the identification of the named parties and are often combined in one numbered paragraph, even though they contain several distinct but related thoughts. The essential parts are (1) that the action is brought as a class action, (2) a definition of the class, and (3) a recitation of the factual elements required for certification. The last part is usually tracked from the language of the rule. FRCP 23. An example under federal practice:

> Plaintiff brings this action as a class action on behalf of all persons located in Michigan who owned a home on or after April 1, 1979, that contained a mortgage issued or owned by State Savings & Loan Association and that contained a due on sale clause. Plaintiff is a member of this class. The class is so numerous that joinder of all members is impracticable. There are questions of law or fact common to the class. The claims of plaintiff as the representative party are typical of the claims of the class. Plaintiff will fairly and adequately protect the interests of the class. Questions of law or fact common to the members of the class predominate over any questions affecting only individ-

ual members, and a class action is superior to other available methods for the fair and efficient adjudication of the controversy.

§ 4.08 ADOPTION BY REFERENCE

Frequently in beginning a new count, a pleader will adopt prior allegations by reference. The traditional cumbersome form is

> Plaintiff realleges and incorporates herein by reference each and every allegation contained in paragraph _____ of the _____ count of the action as if fully set forth.

This may be shortened considerably, with no loss of substantive effect, to read this way:

> Plaintiff adopts by reference paragraphs _____ and _____.

The federal rules contain an express provision for statements to be "adopted by reference." FRCP 10(c). The extra language of the traditional form is unnecessary to effect an adoption, as is the phrase "as if fully set forth" (or a similar phrase). Always state the specific paragraph numbers adopted.

§ 4.09 EXHIBITS

There are two conflicting views about exhibits to a complaint. I share the view that you should *not* have any exhibits to a complaint except when expressly required by court rule.

Several reasons support this. First, matters of evidence do not belong in a complaint, even under fact pleading. Second, courts do not act on complaints alone but rather in response to motions, at which time documents may be introduced as exhibits to an affidavit. Third, exhibits to a complaint are not in evidence as such and must be separately introduced anyway.

Of course, the complaint could be verified, in which case the exhibits would be authenticated. I am not in favor of the verified complaint, however, unless it is expressly required by statute or rule or unless there is simply no time to prepare a separate affidavit, such as a last-minute complaint for immediate injunctive relief.

The opposing view would include exhibits to render a more complete picture of the claim and thus make all of the important documents available for handy reference. But this can be done in other convenient ways. It is also argued that an exhibit requires the defendant at the outset to admit that the copy of the exhibit is a genuine copy. But admissions of the genuineness of a copy are easily obtained in requests to admit and other forms of discovery or by stipulation at pretrial.

The federal rules do not require exhibits to a complaint. The only statement in the rules is "A copy of any written instrument which is an exhibit to a pleading is a part thereof for all purposes." FRCP 10(c).

When an exhibit is a part of a pleading "for all purposes," it is unnecessary to include the kind of language often used in referring to an attached exhibit. For example, traditional language often appears like this:

A copy of the contract is attached hereto as Exhibit A, and made a part hereof by reference, as if fully set forth.

It is sufficient to say:

A copy of the contract is attached as Exhibit A.

Make it easy for the reader to determine where one exhibit ends and another starts. Either use tabs or divider pages, or put the exhibit number on each page. It is frustrating to have to thumb through many multiple-page exhibits (some of which may include their own exhibits) to find a particular exhibit.

§ 4.10 REFERENCES TO STATUTES AND OTHER LEGAL PRINCIPLES

The popular lore is that complaints allege facts only. Yet the court rules, state and federal, require at the very least that the complaint put the defendant on notice of the claim he must defend. Many actions do not require reference to a legal principle. Examples are a suit on a promissory note or for breach of contract. Many other actions, however, are grounded on legal principles that the complaint should set forth, in order to reasonably inform the defendant of the claim. An example is an action by a partner for breach of common law and statutory fiduciary duties. The complaint should contain something in this style:

Defendants owe plaintiffs the following duties:

(a) to grant plaintiff equal rights in the management and conduct of the partnership business. MCLA 449 18(e);

(b) to grant plaintiff access to the partnership books. MCLA 449.19; and

(c) to render on demand true and full information of all things affecting the partnership. MCLA 449.20.

Note that the complaint tracks the statutory text for the nature of the duty. The averment of breach can, of course, similarly track the language.

Example:

Defendants breached the duties owed plaintiff by:

(a) failing to grant plaintiff equal rights. . . .

Some complaints are based on technical statutes or regulations. Those complaints should include references to the sections directly related to the claim. Always include a cross-reference to the compilation, such as USC or CFR. The court and opposing counsel usually have only the compilation. For example, Section 1 of the Sherman Act, 15 USC 1; Section 10b of the Securities Exchange Act, 15 USC 78j(b); Section 301 of the Michigan uniform securities act, MCLA 451.701.

Another situation in which a legal reference is desirable is a factual averment that tracks the standard of a technical provision.

Example:

Defendants failed to disclose the amount of credit that will be paid to the customer, including all charges individually itemized, as required by Regulation Z §226.8(d)(1), 12 CFR 226.8(d)(1).

Another example is the fiduciary duty previously mentioned. *See also* § 4.05 for legal references in jurisdictional averments.

§ 4.11 QUOTATIONS

Quotations are rarely appropriate in a complaint. A key phrase from a contract or other document or a key part of a legal duty can be stated verbatim as part of your complaint paragraph without quotation marks. Or you could have a short quote. For example: "In these circumstances Medicaid requires the state to reimburse the provider for its 'reasonable cost.'" Longer blocked quotations are almost never proper in a complaint.

§ 4.12 DECLARATION OF RIGHTS

The style for seeking declaratory relief should track the style of the applicable rule or statute. See 28 USC 2201.

Example:

There is an actual controversy about whether the loan is usurious and about the amount plaintiff owes. Plaintiff seeks a declaration that

(a) the loan is usurious; and

(b) plaintiff will fully discharge the loan when the total payments to defendant equal the principal amount of $10,000.

§ 4.13 INFORMATION AND BELIEF

When you are pleading a matter on information and belief, simply begin the paragraph "on information and belief . . . ." Don't use stilted preambles such as "plaintiff is informed and believes and upon such information and belief alleges that . . . ."

§ 4.14 DEMAND FOR JUDGMENT

I prefer a single demand for judgment at the end of the complaint, although it is also appropriate (though not required) to include a separate demand at the end of each count. This part of the complaint is popularly called the prayer for relief, although the rules call it a "demand for judgment." FRCP 8(a).

The demand is not as significant as it might seem; for the court rules provide that except for default judgments, "every final judgment shall grant the relief to which the party in whose favor it is rendered is entitled, even if the party has not demanded such relief in his pleadings." FRCP 54(c).

In requesting a money judgment, I have long believed that you should not set forth a specific sum, except possibly when an amount can be readily computed under an instrument. The reasons are several. First, the other side will spend considerable time saying something like, "Okay, you have claimed $1 million in damages, now itemize and explain each element that forms the basis for this amount." Second, the amount, especially if it is large and unliquidated, simply looks like grandstanding. Any defendant collectible for a large amount will not be scared by the prayer. The only arguable excuses for listing a dollar amount are when the client demands it over your objection or when your goal (however misguided) is news media attention. *But see* FRCP 8(a)(3), which requires a demand "for the relief to which he deems himself entitled."

A demand for declaratory relief should set forth the declaration you seek.

Examples:

Declare that the agreement is enforceable

Declare that the defendant has engaged in an unlawful conspiracy in violation of Section 1 of the Sherman Act

A demand for injunctive relief need not identify each person, other than the defendant to be bound. This is provided in the court rules. FRCP 65(d).

Here is a sample demand for judgment that is clear, concise, and adequate:

Plaintiff requests the court:

1. declare the defendant has unlawfully tortiously interfered with plaintiff's contract;

2. preliminarily and permanently enjoin defendant from tortiously interfering with plaintiff's contract;

3. award plaintiff damages in whatever amount it is found to be entitled plus interest;

4. award plaintiff its costs and attorney fees;

5. grant plaintiff such other relief as is just.

Note: By putting the phrase "the court" in the preamble, you need not repeat it in each part of the demand. The general concluding demand in the example is, as previously noted, unnecessary, but it is harmless to include it. Words like "wherefore" and "prays" are not required.

§ 4.15 SIGNATURE

The attorney for a party is the firm, unless the individual attorney is retained apart from his practice with the firm. The rules require that the complaint be signed by an individual attorney, with the implied certification the rules set forth. FRCP 11. The federal rules require the attorney's address. FRCP 11. Also include the telephone number. Sample signature in federal court:

OWEN & SIMON, P.C.

By: _____

John Owen

and: _____

James Associate

2200 Woodward Avenue
Suite 200
Detroit, Michigan 48226
(313) 333-2520
Attorneys for Plaintiff

A party not represented by an attorney must sign his name and list his address as required for attorneys. FRCP 11. It has the implied certification of the rules. FRCP 11.

§ 4.16 VERIFICATION

The plaintiff must verify the complaint only when a statute or rule requires it. FRCP 11. One example in which verification is required would be a shareholder's derivative action in federal courts. FRCP 23.1. A request for ex parte relief, if not supported by a separate affidavit, must have a verified complaint. The plaintiff represented by an attorney may sign any complaint, but he usually signs only a verified complaint. When the "verifier" signs the complaint, this notary is sufficient:

On _____, 198__, _____ who signed this complaint, was sworn and stated that the facts alleged in the complaint are true, except those stated on information and belief he believes true.

[notary signature and
notarial information]

An alternative is a verification by a short affidavit instead of the verifier signing the complaint:

_____, being sworn, says:

1. I am the plaintiff [or the president of plaintiff, *etc.*] in this action.

2. The facts alleged in the complaint are true, except those stated on information and belief I believe are true.

Subscribed and sworn to before

me on _____ _____, 198__

Mary Smith

Notary public

_____

My Commission Expires: _____

This notary will be referred to in this manual as the "short form" notary.

A federal statute also expressly permits the following declaration instead of verification on all pleadings, affidavits, and any other paper that would require a notary:

> I declare under penalty of perjury that the foregoing is true and correct.

> Executed on: _____

28 USC 1746 ("Executed on," rather than "dated," is in the statute).

I recommend the use of declarations. They are simpler, and they do not require the presence of a notary.

§ 4.17 JURY DEMAND

A jury is waived unless the party timely demands it. FRCP 38. Always demand a jury if the action has any "factual" issues. It is far easier to waive it later than to get a jury trial if you did not timely demand it.

The demand may easily appear as part of the party's first pleading, which the rules expressly permit. FRCP 38(b). Put the words "Jury Trial Demanded" in the right side of the caption, below the space for the action number.

A federal court jury demand in pleadings may also appear after the signature (including a second signature) or on a separate paper with a caption.

Example:

JURY DEMAND
Plaintiff demands a jury trial.

[attorney signature]

Some pleaders more cautiously state a jury demand as "Plaintiff demands a jury trial on all issues triable by jury."

§ 4.18 SUMMONS

Although an attorney may draft his own summons, nearly everyone uses printed forms supplied by the court. The rules state the required elements. FRCP 4(b). The official federal forms contain a text for the summons. FRCP Form 1; *see also* FRCP Form 22-A (third party summons).

§ 4.19 AMENDED COMPLAINTS AND AMENDMENTS TO COMPLAINTS

An amended complaint should be a complete text. It supersedes earlier pleadings. 6 WRIGHT AND MILLER,

Federal Practice and Procedure § 1476. Do not incorporate by reference or reallege any part of the earlier complaint. A reader should not have to resort to the prior pleading for anything except historical purposes. An amendment to a complaint, however, makes specific changes or additions, leaving the balance of the prior pleading intact.

Example 1:

AMENDMENT TO COMPLAINT

Plaintiff amends the complaint by adding the following:

COUNT III

12. . . . .

13. . . . .

Example 2:

AMENDMENT TO COMPLAINT

Plaintiff amends the complaint by deleting paragraphs _____ and _____ and the demand for money damages.

(Example 2 may arise when plaintiff wants to pursue equitable issues only.)

When an amendment makes a change, rather than an addition, it should clearly set forth the change.

5

Answers

---

§ 5.01 INTRODUCTION

Many pleading rules and techniques apply to all pleadings. Consequently, many of the sections in the complaint chapter apply equally here. Examples include adoption by reference, jury demand, signature, and exhibits.

§ 5.02 STRUCTURE OF ANSWER

Responses to the averments in the complaint have three basic styles.

Style 1: Respond to each paragraph of the complaint with a corresponding paragraph of the answer, using the same paragraph numbers.

Example:

ANSWER

Defendants answer the complaint as follows:

1. Admit

2. Admit

3. Deny

4. Admit

An alternative version is even easier:

ANSWER

Defendants answer the complaint as follows:

1.-7. Admit

8. Deny

9. Admit

Note the following:

1. It is not necessary to start each paragraph with "The defendant [admits]." This is covered by the introductory clause.

2. Nor is it necessary to repeat in each paragraph answer the corresponding paragraph of the complaint, such as admits "the allegations of paragraph _____." The reader should know that the paragraph numbers in the answer correspond to those in the complaint.

3. The alternative version has the virtue of producing a shorter answer to most lengthy complaints. Often the answer admits many early background averments and denies many later ones. This style is a time-saver.

Style 2: Combine in one paragraph of the answer the response to all consecutive paragraphs of the complaint that have an identical response. The paragraph numbers of the answer do not need to be identical to the complaint paragraphs.

Example:

ANSWER

Defendants answer the complaint as follows:

1. Admit paragraphs 1-3.

2. Deny paragraph 4.

3. Admit paragraph 5.

I used this style for years, but I now prefer style 1 or 3.

Style 3: This combines similar responses to all paragraphs of the complaint in one paragraph of the answer.

Example:

ANSWER

Defendants answer the complaint as follows:

1. Admit paragraphs 1-3 and 5.

2. Deny paragraph 4.

3. Adopt by reference the answers to the allegations adopted by reference in paragraphs . . . .

Responses can be combined only if they are identical. All others must be listed separately. This is often the shortest answer to a lengthy federal complaint. You will have one paragraph for admissions, one for denials, one for lack of knowledge and belief, one for incorporations, plus some special paragraphs that combine two or more of these. The federal forms encourage this style. *See* FRCP Form 20.

§ 5.03 STRUCTURE OF RESPONSE TO AVERMENTS

The federal rules require the pleader to admit, deny, or deny knowledge or information sufficient to form a belief about the truth of an averment. FRCP 8(b). The pleader should use the words set forth in the rules. When a pleader lacks knowledge, a proper response is

6. Without knowledge or information sufficient to form a belief about the truth of the averments.

It is unnecessary to add, "therefore neither admit nor deny" or "leave plaintiff to its proofs." The language of the rule operates as a denial. FRCP 8(b).

How should you respond when part of a numbered paragraph you are answering is true, part is untrue, or in part you lack knowledge? Two principles apply. First, matters not denied are considered admitted. FRCP 8(d). Second, you cannot deny everything if part is true. The federal rules state:

Denials shall fairly meet the substance of the averments denied. When a pleader intends in good faith to deny only a part or a qualification of an averment, he shall specify so much of it as is true and material and shall deny only the remainder. Unless the pleader intends in good faith to controvert all the averments . . . he may make his denials as specific denials of designated averments . . . or he may generally deny all the averments except such designated averments . . . as he expressly admits. . . .

FRCP 8(b).

I recommend the last option of the federal rule, which is to deny everything except for those matters that the pleader admits or denies sufficient knowledge of. This is usually preferable even if the denial is only a minor part of the averment. Make your admissions limited and specific.

Example:

Complaint:

10. A conference was held on May 5, 1980, for the purpose of intimidating plaintiff, and plaintiff felt threatened.

Answer:

10. Denies, except denies knowledge or information sufficient to form a belief about how plaintiff felt, and admits that a conference was held on the date alleged.

A long answer? Perhaps. But pleadings frame the issues.

Many drafters simply deny the allegations in the last example on the theory that if one part of an averment is untrue (the purpose of the conference in this example), you can deny it entirely.

To some extent it is a matter of degree, depending on the structure of the averments. For example, consider an averment of entering into an unlawful agreement. Most attorneys would simply deny this, rather than admit an agreement but deny that it was unlawful. On the other hand, when an averment is structured as a compound of several different facts or thoughts, such as the previous example (the May 5 conference), the rules seem to require precision in the suggested answer.

When the complaint averment simply incorporates other paragraphs, an appropriate answer is

Adopt[s] by reference the answers to the averments adopted by reference in paragraph _____.

§ 5.04 CONVENTIONS IN RESPONSES

Many conventions in responses are in such widespread use that they appear to have tacit acceptance.

One convention is the response to averments summarizing (or quoting) a provision in a document, such as a contract term. The conventional response is to neither admit nor deny because the document is the best evidence of its terms. But this does not comply with the mandate that a pleader admit, deny, or deny knowledge, nor does it further the pleading goal of defining the issues. Yet it appears to be accepted by many judges.

A second convention is the response to statements of law. The response is to neither admit nor deny because it is a conclusion of law, not an averment of fact. This may be proper under the rules. Pleadings are established to narrow factual disputes and to recite legal claims, not to resolve legal claims. For a time I believed the proper response to a statement of a legal principle was to deny knowledge and thereby leave the opposing party with the duty of establishing it. A problem can occur, however, when the plaintiff says something like, "You are a general partner and you didn't know you had a fiduciary duty?" Perhaps "neither admit nor deny" is best.

A somewhat related question is the response to a jurisdictional statement, for example, "This is an action under the civil rights act." My own convention is to deny the allegation but to admit that plaintiff purports to base the claim on the statute alleged.

When an averment concerns acts of the answering defendant and other defendants, you should respond specifically for the answering party, but you may deny knowledge about others if that is accurate.

Example:

> Deny the averments of paragraph 12 as to the answering defendants, except admit defendant Owen Simon wrote the letter referred to, and deny knowledge or information sufficient to form a belief about the truth of the averments as to the nonanswering defendants.

Be careful before admitting any averment. If there is any doubt or if the matter is outside the pleader's direct knowledge, a response other than an admission is appropriate. A useful example is the description of parties. The pleader obviously has knowledge of the averment concerning him. What about another party with whom he does business? Is the pleader absolutely sure a corporation was listed with the exact name on file and the state of incorporation? It is proper to deny knowledge of these items. This is true even if the pleader affirmatively states the same information in a counterclaim or cross-claim. For this purpose, each part of the answer is independent.

§ 5.05 AFFIRMATIVE DEFENSES

The court rules set forth a laundry list of defenses that are waived if not expressly asserted in the answer or preanswer motion. FRCP 8(c), 12(b); 5 WRIGHT AND MILLER, FEDERAL PRACTICE AND PROCEDURE §1278. Always consult this list when preparing an answer, not only to avoid the waiver but also to discover an available defense that you may not have considered.

The list in the rules is not exhaustive. Under the federal rules the answer must also include "any other matter constituting an avoidance or affirmative defense." FRCP 8(c).

My preferred format is this: The affirmative defenses should immediately follow the responses to the paragraphs of the complaint. The rules require separately numbered paragraphs. FRCP 10(b). The affirmative defenses should be in numbered paragraphs continuing the prior numbering (rather than starting with number one). The reasons for continuing the numbering are that the affirmative defenses are part of one document called an "answer" and that this avoids having more than one paragraph with the same number.

The defenses should be preceded by a general heading, "Affirmative Defenses," or, alternatively, each paragraph should be preceded by a specific heading, for example, "First Affirmative Defense," "Second Affirmative Defense," and so forth. If one or more affirmative defenses has more than one numbered paragraph, use specific headings to separate the different defenses.

Example:

FIRST AFFIRMATIVE DEFENSE

16.

17.

SECOND AFFIRMATIVE DEFENSE

18.

THIRD AFFIRMATIVE DEFENSE

19.

What is the amount of detail required? For example, is it sufficient to say the claim is "barred by estoppel," or must the pleader generally recite the reliance and change of position? Federal defenses must be "in short and plain terms." FRCP 8(b). In practice, a barebones notice of the defense is usually sufficient, leaving the details for discovery. The better practice, however, is to give the same specificity for all defenses that is required for averments in complaints. The kinds of matters that must be stated with particularity in complaints should be similarly asserted when they are part of affirmative defenses. *E.g.,* FRCP 9(b).

When you intend to rely on an affirmative defense that is not asserted in the answer, the proper course is to move to amend the answer to allege it. You cannot assume that it will seep into the action as an issue tried with the implied consent of the parties. *See* FRCP 15(b). Defenses asserted in preanswer motions need not be repeated in an answer. FRCP 12(b).

§ 5.06 RESERVATION OF DEFENSES

Many answers include a section similar to this:

RESERVATION OF DEFENSES
Defendants reserve the right to raise additional affirmative defenses after discovery.

Regrettably, even some large law firms routinely add this. The statement is meaningless and inappropriate. All defenses must be raised in the answer or by pre-answer motion. FRCP 12(b). Leave to amend and add defenses is "freely given when justice so requires." FRCP 15(a). Some defenses are forever waived. FRCP 12(h). Parties cannot unilaterally enlarge their position by a self-serving reservation of defenses. Putting someone on general notice adds nothing.

§ 5.07 COUNTERCLAIMS AND CROSS-CLAIMS

These pleadings may be in a separate document but are more often inserted in the answer after the affirmative defenses, with a new heading, and a continuation of the paragraph numbers in the answer. The pleadings were traditionally considered to be part of the answer and can be considered as a "defense" to the complaint if that is appropriate. FRCP 13 and 8(c); FRCP Form 20.

One style, which I call the "long form," is an independent pleading that can stand alone with the full panoply of averments of a complaint. This includes the allegation of jurisdiction, identifying parties, and the full factual outline required in a complaint showing the pleader is entitled to relief. The federal rules contemplate this long form. A compulsory federal counterclaim needs no independent jurisdictional basis. In this case you need not expressly aver jurisdiction, FRCP Form 20, but some courts require it anyway. The long form is also preferred for complicated federal cross-claims.

The "short form" draws on the allegations of the complaint and sets forth the minimum averments of notice of the claim.

Example:

CROSS-CLAIM

1. Defendant general contractor entered into a subcontract with defendant subcontractor for the construction of a sewer line along Main Street in the area of the Riverview Apartments.

2. The complaint seeks damages for injuries to plaintiff on _____ from a fall in the area of defendant subcontractor's work.

3. Defendant general contractor did not cause or contribute to plaintiff's injuries.

4. The conditions plaintiff complains about were created solely by defendant subcontractor.

[Defendant general contractor] demands judgment against [defendant subcontractor] for any amount judgment enters against [defendant general contractor] in favor of plaintiff.

(Substitute parties' names within these brackets.)

In these pleadings do not use terms such as "counterplaintiff" or "cross-defendant." These names only add gibberish. Use the party's proper name, or if there are few parties, you can use the original terms "plaintiff" and "defendant," even though the roles are reversed.

§ 5.08 THIRD-PARTY CLAIMS

Third-party complaints by a defendant (or by a plaintiff as to a counterclaim) are generally governed by the same pleading rules as other affirmative pleadings. FRCP 14. You must also serve a summons on the new party. *See* FRCP Form 22-A. Whether you must move to file the third-party complaint is governed by court rule. Normally the original complaint is attached as an exhibit. Then, set forth the third-party claim and demand for judgment. The cross-claim example in the last section may also serve as an example of a third-party complaint if it is preceded by the following:

THIRD-PARTY COMPLAINT

1. Plaintiff _____ has filed a complaint against defendant [general contractor]. A copy is attached as Exhibit A.

Since the third-party complaint must satisfy a complaint's pleading rules, it should state enough to show that you are entitled to relief. In federal practice you may adopt by reference appropriate portions of the original complaint attached to the third-party complaint. You need not allege jurisdiction in third-party practice.

§ 5.09 PRAYER FOR RELIEF

Most answers contain a prayer for relief, although the rules do not require it.

Example:

> Defendant requests that the court dismiss the complaint with prejudice and award defendants costs and attorney fees.

Note: It is unnecessary to state that costs and attorney fees were "wrongfully sustained." When the answer includes other pleadings, such as a counterclaim or cross-claim, the answer must, of course, include a demand for judgment seeking affirmative relief as in a complaint.

6

Motion Practice

§ 6.01 INTRODUCTION

Motion practice includes a variety of papers: the motion and notice of hearing, affidavit, brief, proof of service, opposition papers, and the court order. The only paper universally required is the motion itself, although the prevailing party or the court will presumably want an order.

The notice of hearing is required in many federal courts, even if the court sets the date.

Affidavits are generally needed only to supplement a factual record if necessary. Certain kinds of motions require them, such as preliminary injunctions (unless the complaint is verified) or disqualification of the judge. The federal rules state a summary judgment motion grounded on a lack of a genuine issue of fact may be "with or without supporting affidavits." FRCP 56(a).

Briefs are required by local rule in many federal districts and under many state rules. Briefs are discussed in a later chapter.

Proof of service is required by local rule in some districts.

§ 6.02 MOTIONS

The court rules require that the motion set forth the ground on which it is based "with particularity" and set forth "the relief or order sought." FRCP 7(b)(1). When supported by an explanatory brief or affidavit, the motion itself can be brief. *See, e.g,* FRCP Form 19. If the motion is based on a court rule, I prefer to cite it. You should recite the standard from the involved rule, such as the familiar phrases relating to failure to state a claim or lack of genuine factual issue. You should then generally refer to the specific ground.

When the motion is for summary judgment because no genuine issue of fact exists, there is no more specific ground except that the issue of fact should be identified.

Local rules in some federal courts require a statement that the movant has contacted the other side. Again, follow the text of the applicable rule.

Example:

MOTION TO DISMISS
Defendant moves to dismiss under FRCP 12(b)(6) because the complaint fails to state a claim upon which

relief can be granted. The instrument plaintiff sues on is not a security and, therefore, no claim exists under the securities laws.

[insert concurrence of counsel language]

This motion is supported by an accompanying brief.

By way of contrast, this is one style of some prior forms:

MOTION TO DISMISS

Now comes, _____ defendant in the above entitled cause, and moves this Honorable Court for an order of dismissal and shows as follows:

1.

2.

This motion is based on the record and files herein.

Wherefore, your defendant prays this Honorable Court enter an order dismissing the complaint.

Apart from the old-fashioned style, several points are worth noting:

1. As explained earlier, it is unnecessary to add the phrase "defendant in the above entitled cause" to any court paper. Simply name the party or say "defendant[s]" or "defendant[s] _____."

2. It is superfluous to say that something is "based on the record and files." Everything a court does is based on that.

3. It is not necessary to include a separate prayer for relief. The relief requested should appear in the beginning of the motion.

Multiple or alternative motions may be in one document.

Example:

MOTION TO DISMISS
OR FOR CHANGE OF VENUE

Defendants move as follows:

1. To dismiss under FRCP 12(b)(2) for lack of personal jurisdiction.

2. Alternatively, to change venue to the District of Columbia under 28 USC 1404 for the convenience of parties and witnesses, in the interest of justice.

or

Defendants move to dismiss under . . . .

If that motion is denied, defendants alternatively move . . . .

Arguably, the rules require that all motions, affidavits, and other papers have separately numbered paragraphs. FRCP 7(b)(2) and 10(b). But even the official forms do not include numbered paragraphs for short motions. *E.g.,* FRCP Form 22-B. The practice, especially in federal court, is often not to use numbered paragraphs even in longer motions.

§ 6.03 NOTICE OF HEARING

This paper is simply an announcement of when the motion is scheduled for argument. It should be brief. Contrast these styles.

Old style:

NOTICE OF HEARING

To _____

Attorney For _____

Please take notice that the motion for _____
_____ will be brought on for hearing
before the Honorable _____ in his
courtroom in the _____ County
Courthouse, in the City of _____, on
_____, or as soon thereafter as coun-
sel may be heard.

Suggested style:

NOTICE OF HEARING
The motion for _____ is set for argument in the courtroom of Judge _____
_____ on _____, at
9:00 a.m. [, or as soon as the clerk calls the matter.]

The part in brackets, a holdover from the old style,
is optional.

Apart from the plain style of the suggested form,
note that it is not addressed to opposing counsel. Although found in many form books, that convention is
unnecessary. Every paper served and filed in an action
is "addressed" to all parties. (The summons is the only
paper the rules require to be addressed to the party.
FRCP 4(b).)

Nor is it necessary to describe the location, by building or city, of the judge's courtroom. If the other parties don't know where the courthouse is, they are in
real trouble.

Sometimes the rule requires a notice of hearing even
though the court sets the hearing date later. The following form is suggested:

NOTICE OF HEARING
The motion for _____will be heard at
a date and time to be fixed by the court.

The notice of hearing may be combined with the motion in the same paper. FRCP 7(b)(1); FRCP Form 19. To do this, just title the paper "Motion and Notice of Hearing" and add the notice information as a separate paragraph.

§ 6.04 AFFIDAVIT

The affidavit format should minimize formalities.

Suggested form:

AFFIDAVIT

[or Affidavit of _____]

State of _____)

_____ County)

_____, being sworn, says:

1. I am the president of defendant _____ _____. I make this affidavit in support of defendant's motion for _____.
I am fully familiar with the facts stated in this affidavit and, if sworn as a witness, I am competent to testify to them.

2. . . .

3. . . .

[signature]

[short form notary]

Note the following about this form:

1. There is no "ss." Whatever meaning it had long ago, it is meaningless today.

2. The introduction is shortened from the stilted "_____, first being duly sworn, deposes and says." The notary signifies that the affiant was "duly" sworn. And if it wasn't "duly" done, that self-serving statement will not help.

3. The text is in the first person "I," and not the third person "he."

4. The phrase "further deponent saith not" may sound quaint, but it is useless. When the reader reaches the signature, he is likely to figure out that the affiant has nothing more to say in that affidavit.

The last sentence in the first paragraph is inserted to satisfy the court rule that the affidavit affirmatively show that the affiant is competent to testify to the facts stated there. FRCP 56(e) (summary judgments). It will also highlight to the affiant and to you the proper limits of an affidavit. Motions are frequently supported by the affidavit of the attorney. These do not satisfy this rule in many instances.

The court rules also generally require the affidavit to include as exhibits all papers referred to there, or to serve them concurrently. FRCP 56(e).

The following are a few rules about style:

1. Make the tone less formal and more conversational than other legal papers. After all, the affidavit is, in theory, the statement of a layman, not a lawyer.

2. Organize the material chronologically or in the logical order of the issues, for example, discuss

liability before relief. In a lengthy affidavit use subject headings to assist the reader. The argument, in the brief or oral, may rearrange the order of the points for emphasis and persuasion. The affidavit places facts in the record from which the attorney crafts the argument. It is a source document.

3. Use a persuasive writing style when appropriate. The judge will read the affidavit. But do not cross the fine line into mere argument. When this happens, the affiant is not stating matters about which he can competently testify. Even worse, it may lessen the persuasiveness of the affidavit.

Persuasive affidavit style is primarily for discretionary matters, such as a preliminary injunction. It is obviously not for pro forma matters, such as an affidavit of nonmilitary service. Nor does it seem appropriate for a summary judgment motion based on a lack of a genuine factual issue The court's role here is limited to determining whether a fact issue exists. If it does, the court must deny the motion. The court does not resolve the issue.

§ 6.05 PROOF OF SERVICE

Here is a suggested proof of service:

State of Michigan)

Oakland County)

Owen Simon, being sworn, states:

I served a copy of _____ on the following persons by placing the document in postage prepaid envelopes addressed to them at their respective addresses and depositing the envelopes in the United States mail in _____

_____, Michigan on _____,
19__:

[names and addresses]

_____
Owen Simon

[short form notary]

A proof of personal service can simply state:

State of Michigan)

Oakland County)

Owen Simon, being sworn, states: On _____,
198__ I personally served a copy of _____ on:

[names and addresses]

_____
Owen Simon

[short form notary]

Alternatively, here is a "form" a secretary can complete that may save time:

State of Michigan)

Oakland County)

The undersigned, being sworn, states he served papers as follows:

1. Document served: [insert]

2. Served on: [insert]

3. Method of Service: ( ) personal service
                                      ( ) first class mail

( ) certified mail,
return receipt requested

4. Date served: [insert]

_____ Owen Simon

[short form notary]

Some attorneys use a stamp placed on the last page or attach a printed form. This can eliminate the need to identify the paper or the persons served. Here is an example of a declaration without a notary, using an alternative style to the affidavit form:

> I served a copy of this document on the attorneys of record of all parties by mailing a copy to them at their respective business addresses as disclosed by the record, with postage fully prepaid on _____, 198___. I declare that the statements above are true to the best of my information, knowledge and belief.

See the discussion of declarations in 4.16.

§ 6.06 ORDERS

Court orders on motions contribute an unbelievable amount of gibberish. They confirm Mellinkoff's statement that some legal writing is not written for anyone; it is written just to be written.

Let's start with "at a session of . . . ." This is used by custom by some federal judges.

Standard style:

> At a session of said Court held in the courthouse in the
> City of _____, County of
> _____ on the _____ day of
> _____, 198__.

You don't talk like that, so don't write like that. Suggested form:

> At a session of court held in the courthouse in _____
> _____, Michigan on _____, 198__.

The recitals are generally even more stilted. The standard style:

> Defendant having filed a motion for summary
> judgment, the plaintiff having filed a brief in op-
> position thereto, the matter having come on for
> hearing, the court being fully advised in the
> premises, and the court having denied the mo-
> tion, now therefore
>
>   IT IS HEREBY ORDERED . . . .

Even the official federal forms fall into this trap. *See*
FRCP Forms 31-32.

Suggested style:

> Defendant moved for summary judgment. The parties
> filed briefs and the court heard argument. The court
> decided to deny the motion for the reasons stated in the
> bench opinion [or written opinion] of _____
> _____, 198__.
>
>   IT IS ORDERED . . . .

Note the following:

1. The suggested form is not one long assemblage of "having" clauses. It has sentences, with subjects and verbs.

2. The form omits the "fully advised in the premises." What does that nonsense mean? Whatever it may mean, this self-serving statement inserted by the prevailing party adds nothing. The record and court reasoning alone determine whether the order will be upheld.

3. The suggested form does not try to summarize the court's reasoning. Attorneys very often get bogged down in negotiating a summary of the opinion. Don't try. Simply incorporating the opinion eliminates that problem. For better or worse, the court's opinion is what it is. An exception is an injunction, which must "set forth the reasons for its issuance." FRCP 65(d).

The operative portion of the order can be simplified. First, it is unnecessary ever to say:

It is hereby ordered, adjudged and decreed . . . .

A simple "It is ordered" will do the job. When the order has several provisions, you may say:

It is ordered:

1.

2.

3.

You need not repeat "It is further ordered" in each paragraph.

Don't say:

It is ordered that the motion be, and it hereby is, granted.

Instead say:

It is ordered the motion is granted.

The "order" should not include matters covered by court rule unless the judge is ordering something different from the rule. For example, the rules state the time period for a responsive pleading after notice of the denial of a preanswer motion. FRCP 12(a). But the court may alter the time fixed by the rules. FRCP 6(b). Similarly, whether a dismissal is "with prejudice" or "without prejudice" is governed by the rules. FRCP 41. The appropriate modifier is required only if the intention is to deviate from the rule. In these matters, as always, check the rule.

A motion seeking final or specific relief, if granted, should include both the disposition of the motion and the final relief.

Examples:

It is ordered the motion for summary judgment is granted and the complaint is dismissed.

It is ordered the motion for sanctions is granted and the affirmative defense of waiver is stricken. [This example is from FRCP 37(b)(2)(c).]

§ 6.07 PARTIAL JUDGMENTS

Be careful about the text of judgments, such as partial summary judgments, for less than all of the claims or all of the parties. Depending on the text, the judgment may be interlocutory, subject to revision, and not appealable, or it may be final and appealable of right, with the time to appeal starting immediately. FRCP 54(b).

Only the following language, or something substantially similar, will make the judgment final:

The court expressly determines that there is no just reason for delay and expressly directs the entry of this judgment.

This sentence should appear at the end of the recitals. Alternatively, it may be an "It is ordered" clause.

Often the parties will differ about whether the judgment should be final. Consciously determine your position each time and pursue it. Another rule to remember is that in order to be final, every judgment in federal court must be on a separate document. FRCP 58.

§ 6.08 ORDER TO SHOW CAUSE

The concept of an order to show cause in motion practice is both misleading and an anachronism. It is really nothing more than a court-ordered hearing date (which may be sooner than the rules otherwise provide for motions). The order is more accurately an "order fixing the hearing date" or a "scheduling order." It does not shift the burden of proof. It should not shift the burden of going forward. You should not use an order to show cause in the federal courts.

Suggested style:

ORDER SCHEDULING HEARING ON MOTION FOR PRELIMINARY INJUNCTION

Plaintiffs have filed a complaint seeking a declaration that defendant may not accelerate the balance due under a mortgage and may not foreclose based on the acceleration. To protect the rights of plaintiffs relating to the mortgage, they have moved for an injunction preventing defendant from taking any action to foreclose the mortgage on the property involved in this action. Plaintiffs have requested an early hearing date on the motion for a preliminary injunction The court has reviewed the complaint, motion, supporting affidavit, and brief and is persuaded to enter the following order.

1. The motion for a preliminary injunction is set for argument on _____, 198__ at _____ _____ [AM or PM].

2. A copy of the summons, complaint, motion, affidavit, brief, and this order shall be served on defendant by _____, 198__.

3. Defendant shall serve and file with the court its responsive brief and all other papers in opposition to the motion for a preliminary injunction by _____ _____, 198__.

§ 6.09 PRELIMINARY INJUNCTION AND TEMPORARY RESTRAINING ORDERS

This is an example of a motion tightly governed by court rule. FRCP 65. The motion and order must address certain matters. Additional matters must be addressed in ex parte restraining orders. Many orders are set aside because of noncompliance with a technical detail. Read the rule each time you prepare the papers. The rule is your checklist. The following example is a suggested style:

EX PARTE TEMPORARY RESTRAINING
ORDER AND
ORDER SCHEDULING HEARING
[session of the court section
if appropriate in that court]

Plaintiff has filed a complaint and an affidavit verifying the complaint. The court has reviewed these documents. Paragraph ___ of the complaint states:

> Plaintiff will be damaged and suffer substantial injury to its credit standing, future ability to obtain credit, and to its business unless defendant Simon is enjoined from attempting to negotiate the letter of credit and defendant ABC National Bank is enjoined from honoring the letter of credit. If the letter of credit is negotiated, the injury to plaintiff will be irreparable and is one for which there is no adequate remedy at law. Defendant Simon has stated to plaintiff that he intends to negotiate the letter of credit.

It appears to the court that it is necessary to issue an ex parte restraining order to preserve the status quo for these reasons. It appears that the defendants may negotiate the letter of credit at any time, such as after any advance notice that plaintiff would seek this order. It also appears plaintiff will be immediately and irreparably injured in its credit standing, future ability to obtain credit, and its business if the letter of credit is negotiated or paid. Plaintiff will have no adequate remedy at law.

IT IS ORDERED:

1. Defendant Simon is enjoined from attempting to negotiate the ABC National bank letter of credit No. 23889 until the further order of this court.

2. ABC National Bank is enjoined from accepting for payment, negotiating, or paying any funds on its letter of credit No. 23889 concerning plaintiff until the further order of this court.

3. The injunctive relief against Simon and ABC National Bank is binding, in accordance with FRCP 65(d) upon these defendants, their officers, agents, servants, employees, and attorneys and upon all persons in active concert or participation with them who receive actual notice of this order by personal service or otherwise.

4. Security is not required for issuing this restraining order because the letter of credit to which the order relates is sufficient security for any costs or damages that may be incurred or suffered by any party who is found to have been wrongfully enjoined or restrained or any other party.

5. The motion for a preliminary injunction is set for argument on _____, 198___, at [AM or PM].

6. A copy of the summons, complaint, motion, affidavit, brief, and this order shall be served on defendants on or before _____, 198___. Plaintiff shall file a proof of service.

This order is issued on _____, 198___, at _____ [AM or PM].

Note the following:

1. The rule requires that the verified complaint or affidavit clearly state by specific facts why the order must issue ex parte. Similarly, the order must define the injury, state why it is irreparable, and state why the order was granted without notice. FRCP 65(b).

2. If the verified complaint or affidavit is properly drafted, the order can quote it as in the example. This serves several purposes: It shows that the complaint or affidavit satisfies the rule; it places all of the relevant material in the order itself; it saves drafting time; and it assists the court in making the required findings in the order.

3. The rules also require the plaintiff's attorney to state in writing the efforts to give notice or the reasons that it is not necessary. This separate requirement is not part of the order. FRCP 65(b).

4. The federal rules require security for costs "in such sum as the court deems proper" if the injunction is later found improper. FRCP 65(c).

5. The portion of the example reciting the persons bound by the order is technically unnecessary, since the rule states that these people are bound. FRCP 65(d). In fact, the text of the example quotes the rule. Including this material is an exception to the general principle that you omit matters covered by rule. The reason is that injunctive relief is so critical, and because the order is often served on nonlawyers about to take imminent action, that extra caution is proper.

6. The rule requires every injunction be specific and describe the acts enjoined, without reference to another document. FRCP 65(d). The example refers to the letter of credit by its number.

7. The order must state the date and hour of issuance. The motion must be scheduled for hearing at the earliest possible time. FRCP 65(b).

A preliminary injunction differs little from an ex parte order. It need not include the reasons that the relief is ex parte and the harm irreparable. Yet every injunction must "set forth the reasons for its issuance." FRCP 65(d). Although there appears to be more leeway when the order is not ex parte, the general style should be similar. The only other differences in the orders are that a non-ex parte order need not state the date and hour of issuance (it will always state the date anyway) and, of course, it need not set a further hearing or require service of papers.

7

Briefs

§ 7.01 INTRODUCTION

No lawsuit paper is more important than the brief. The record consists of all other papers: pleadings, discovery papers, motions and affidavits, stipulations, and others. The brief organizes the record and the law to persuade the judge that you should win the contested point the brief discusses. The brief is the keystone.

Never forget that the sole purpose of the brief is to persuade the judge. The issue may be life and death to the parties, but it is usually just part of a day's work to the judge. Like everyone else, a judge has plenty to do. The brief must first get the judge's attention, and then, it must persuade. Always ask yourself: Would I read this brief? Would I be persuaded? The following rules should help you.

1. *Write in a plain style so that a nonlawyer can understand what it is about.* My rule is that if my wife or secretary cannot understand the basic issue by reading my brief, I rewrite. Very few legal issues are so complex that they cannot be explained in English. The words should be for laymen even if the detail is for lawyers.

Many lawyers can explain an issue plainly and concisely at a cocktail party but will write the brief incoherently. Without being too colloquial, draft the setting for the brief as you would explain it to a friend.

2. *Keep it short.* A judge, like anyone else, is more likely to read the brief if it is crisp. Except for a short introduction, do not repeat a point. Some briefs should be 50 or more pages, for example, when a brief discusses many issues and therefore is really several "briefs." Most briefs should be far shorter. Do not be embarrassed by a two-page brief if two pages says it all.

Write important briefs or sections of briefs in longhand. You can almost always spot a brief dictated into a machine by the extra words. Longhand results in many fewer words and much less repetition.

Put aside the completed brief as long as you can. Then read it again and cut generously. Let go of unneeded material, even if you think it is your best handiwork.

Some successful attorneys use the opposite style. One attorney I know always files laboriously long briefs, with endless quotes often exceeding a page.

The same point is made over and over. The theory of this tour de force style is that eventually the judge will get the point. You tell the judge what you will say, you say it, and then you tell him what you said.

This style also attempts to intimidate the judge. How can he rule contrary to such a massive tome? This style may work for some, but it is contrary to the theme of this manual.

3. *State the rule or conclusion first.* In each part of your legal analysis, give the bottom line first, plainly and without fanfare. Then give the support. This sequence will let the reader know what to look for as you engage in a maze of citation and argument. A good judge could even skim the detail with this roadmap marked out. A novel leaves the climax for the end. In this respect, a brief is the opposite of a novel.

4. *Use Headings.* Separate different elements of the facts or arguments with headings. They may be neutral but, especially sub-headings, may be argumentative.

5. *Omit extreme rhetoric.* A seasoned judge will not only ignore extreme rhetoric, he may even consider rhetoric a mask for lack of a strong position. Your opponent may even turn it against you. See the examples in 7.14. Avoid statements such as "Plaintiff's case is the weakest claim I have seen in my years of practice." Avoid superlatives.

In many cases the difference between good advocacy and extreme rhetoric is difficult to define. Again, some lawyers are comfortable and successful with heavy rhetoric, but generally it hurts more than it helps.

6. *Avoid "clearly," "obviously," and similar words.* These words are often inserted when the point is not clear or obvious. Most judges are not so easily fooled. When the matter is clear, you need not add such words. Your statement of the principle and your backup demonstrate that the matter is clear.

7. *Be complete.* Your briefs should be so complete that after he reads all the briefs, the judge need only reread yours in deciding the issue and drafting any opinion. Your main and reply briefs collectively, if you are the proponent of the matter, or your responsive brief, if you are the respondent, should succinctly and completely address the other side's position. The judge will appreciate having everything in one place. This helps to neutralize your opponent. Your ultimate goal is for the judge to plagiarize your brief in the opinion.

The sections that follow amplify these points and give other tips, with these caveats. The emphasis is on trial court briefs. Much of the material is also useful for appellate briefs. However, the court rules dictate the basic structure of appellate briefs. *See, e.g.,* FR App P 28. Since this manual is about style, this chapter does not discuss how to research or what substantive material you should include in the brief.

§ 7.02 INTRODUCTORY PARAGRAPH OF BRIEF

The beginning of a brief in a trial court should always tell the judge succinctly what the action and the briefs are about. Do not clutter this overview with technical descriptions of the parties, the facts, or the law. The body of the brief will do that.

The opening paragraph of a short brief need only give the setting; presumably, the judge will fully read a short brief.

Examples:

> This is an action by a borrower claiming violations of the usury and consumer protection statutes. The borrower has moved to enjoin the foreclosure of the mortgage. This brief is in opposition to [or in support of] that motion.

> This is an action by a contractor, ABC, based on anticipatory breach of a contract to construct a sewer when the contractor was ordered to stop work. The answer asserts the defense of impossibility because of a rescission of a federal environmental permit. This brief is in support of ABC's motion to dismiss that affirmative defense.

The description of the nature of the action in the same or modified form can be used in other briefs in the action on other issues. I generally start a brief with a description of the action even when the judge has become thoroughly familiar with it.

The opening paragraph of a long brief should advocate your position. Again, your goals are to make the judge want to read your full brief and to predispose him to your position.

The beginning of a long brief is often critical. It should be your highest quality work. Rewrite it several times more than the rest of your brief.

Do not summarize all your points. Select those you believe have the greatest practical or legal appeal. Often your best emotional fact, which you should include here, may not be the most legally significant.

Pretend you have the judge's undivided attention on the matter for only 30 seconds. In that time, say what you want the judge to know. Consider the following example from a truth-in-lending action:

> The question presented by this class certification motion is whether plaintiff's attorney can finance and prosecute a class action for a nominal plaintiff who cannot pay any costs herself and does not understand the claims in the lawsuit. Even if plaintiff is correct on all her claims, the fact remains she received for her benefit loan proceeds of $6,600, has made no payments in a year and a half, and is unable to make up her deficiencies. As an individual, plaintiff could recover a statutory penalty of $1,000. As a class representative, she can receive $6 at most. It is against plaintiff's economic interest to have a class certified. The only major recovery in a class action would be to plaintiff's lawyer for larger statutory attorney fees. Because this is an abuse of the class action rule, defendant opposes class certification.

§ 7.03 FACT STATEMENT

The statement of facts should have these elements. It should be as complete as is necessary for the court to apply the legal principles you discuss and those your opponent has discussed (or you know he will discuss). It should be neutral, not argumentative. Avoid legal conclusions. Make sure all facts are in the record or are subject to judicial notice. File an affidavit for any facts not in the record. In an important brief cite to the record after each fact.

Examples:

Complaint ¶10

Simon Dep 10

Rose Aff, Ex E, p3

P1 Interrog Ans No. 16

Bench Opinion 10/12/82

Usually the facts should be chronological. However, it is sometimes better to collect all facts on a side issue in one place.

§ 7.04 ORDER OF LEGAL POINTS

Although the order in which you discuss the legal issues is very important, no single rule governs all situations. A widely accepted format for the main brief is to argue the strongest point first. This is subject to major exceptions.

Serious arguments claiming that the court cannot reach the substantive issue should precede discussion of the substantive issue. The most frequent such argument is lack of subject matter jurisdiction over the dispute. Another is that even if the defendant did not comply with a statute, no private right of action exists. A brief that puts these threshold issues last exposes them as weak.

But sometimes these points will have more force after the substantive analysis, or they may depend on it. Then they should go last. Abstention or a stay of proceedings may be examples.

Liability issues usually precede relief issues. The judge will not consider relief unless liability is established. This is true even in preliminary injunctions, in which the movant need only show a likelihood of success.

A section outlining the procedural test should precede the application of the test. Examples are an analysis of the scope of review of agency action or summary judgment standards.

The main brief seeking an order governed by an established multipart test should address each element in the recognized order of the test. For example, a brief supporting a preliminary injunction should have its points in this order: (1) likelihood of success, (2) irreparable harm, (3) balance of hardships, and (4) public interest. Another example is a class action brief. The proponent should discuss the elements in the order they appear in the rule and caselaw.

When several points are equally forceful, these guidelines should help. One method is to start with the broadest, most complex issues and end with the narrowest. The broadest issues often discuss more facts and better prepare the reader for the narrower ones, which may then be stated even more briefly. Often a reader concentrates more in the early parts of the brief. Presumably, the broad complex issues require the most concentration.

Equally forceful points have a logical progression. For example, you may first argue that the opponent can never do what he has done. Then, building on that, you argue that even if he sometimes can, he cannot do so in the particular context of this action. Fallback or alternative theories follow the main one.

When the brief contains constitutional and nonconstitutional claims, two contrary methods exist. Under the principle that courts do not decide constitutional claims unless they must, argue the nonconstitutional claims first. On the other hand, many good briefs start with the constitutional issues because they are the broadest and most interesting.

The responsive brief is governed by different guidelines. If you have no particular tactical preference, judges appreciate points following the same order as the main brief. But do not feel bound by that. If you do not follow the order of the main brief, try to acknowledge this and explain why. For example, "Because the agreement lacked consideration, we consider that point first."

First and foremost, you want to win. Put your best winning argument first. Although the proponent has to make a showing on every point, the opponent frequently needs to win only on one element of the proponent's burden or on one defense to prevail.

The responsive brief may not even challenge some of the elements. Start with your best, whether it is relief rather than liability or the merits rather than jurisdiction.

However, when the responsive brief opposes each part or most parts of a prescribed test, it is usually better to follow the accepted order. Even here you may put one element first, out of turn, if it is particularly strong.

§ 7.05 STRUCTURE OF EACH POINT

Your legal analysis should progress from the broad to the specific. Often you will begin with a short summary of the general rule or standard. If the test is in the alternative, state at the outset which parts apply and which do not. Judicial or legislative statements of intent or interpretation that support your position follow the general principle. For example: "This statute must be construed broadly to protect the employee." Then review the specific points at issue.

The authorities you cite to support a particular point should follow this order: the highest court and then the intermediate court binding on your court, your court, other courts, and then secondary authorities, usually with the most authoritative first. I follow this order even when the judge hearing the issue (or a close colleague) wrote a prior opinion on point. Mention the name of the judge in citations to decisions of the same trial court. When the opinion of a sister court, not binding in the action, is written by a celebrated judge, try to use that judge's name. For example: "As Judge Hand said . . . ." In other circumstances the judge's name serves no purpose in discussing other sister court opinions.

The order of authorities has its exceptions. The principle from a restatement or a celebrated treatise should be advanced earlier in the discussion especially when it addresses the point and the caselaw is sketchy. Contracts and torts issues may have this tendency.

Statutory issues require a modified approach. Any discussion of the text of the statutory scheme and any involved agency rule precede the caselaw. Legislative history or agency interpretation precedes the caselaw if it is more on point than the opinions and if it is persuasive. If not, include it later, introduced by something like "[T]he legislative history confirms this result."

§ 7.06 TOPIC SENTENCES

The topic sentence of the paragraph is the indispensable working tool of the brief writer. Legal analysis contains tedious detail. It is most readable when the first sentence of the paragraph has these characteristics:

First, the sentence tells the reader succinctly what the paragraph is about. This is the application in the trenches of the general rule that you help the reader by stating the result before the detailed backup.

Second, and even more important, the topic sentences by themselves tell a coherent story. The topic sentence should focus on its relationship to other topic sentences. The reader should be able to understand the guts of the brief simply by skimming the topic sentences.

The balance of each paragraph is, conceptually, a footnote to its topic sentence. Sometimes a reader needs the information in the "footnote" because the topic sentence is general in order to be a topic sentence. But, usually, the reader would not need to read the balance of the paragraph to understand the point it makes or its subject.

Examples:

Preliminary injunctions issue only when the plaintiff meets the following burden.

———————————

The contract shows an intent to follow Michigan law in other ways.

———————————

The statute does not even hint preemption was intended and, if anything, supports no preemption.

Marketplace practices graphically show there is no dominant federal interest requiring national uniformity.

Many of the decisions plaintiff cited, upon examination, do not really help plaintiff

---

Simon is distinguishable from, and consistent with, the later *Rose* opinion.

If *Simon* cannot be distinguished, it is simply wrong.

Avoid starting the topic sentence with a citation. The important material is the legal conclusion, *not* the case name. Making the citation prominent makes it harder to locate the point.

Example:

Wrong: In *Simon v. Rose,* 654 F2d 1001 (CA 6 1981), the court of appeals said the statute must be strictly construed.

Correct: The statute must be strictly construed. *Simon v. Rose,* 654 F2d 1001 (CA 6 1981).

This is a good rule even when the doctrine is named for the case. However, you might then refer to the case in stating the doctrine.

Example:

The Supreme Court held in *Miranda* that . . . . [citation]

When citing added support for a rule already stated, the important point is still the *support,* not the case name.

Examples:

The ninth circuit reached the same result when the employee had an even stronger case. [citation]

Other states concur. [citations]

A New Jersey case confirms that such relief is granted only in cases of extreme hardship. [citation]

A good example of the application of this rule is the sixth circuit decision in . . . .

A good technique is to state a rule or theme and then cite all cases in full that you will discuss. You can begin your later paragraphs with a short citation.

Example:

The courts have readily rejected class action status in situations involving so many individual issues. [citations]

Simon was also a franchise case.

Another good example is *Rose.*

Within a paragraph it is objectionable (but less so) to start a sentence with a citation. The reader is already in the domain of detail. For example, if the topic sentence is something like "Other states concur," the internal sentence could start with a citation. I often introduce a blocked quotation within a paragraph with

the full citation. "In . . . the court said:" In that case
the reader should be focusing on the blocked portion
anyway.

Occasionally, it helps the reader if you number your
points. Consider this when you have several specific
reasons to support a result. Especially consider it if
one or more of the specific reasons requires several
paragraphs. That way the reader will know when you
have switched to a new reason.

Example:

> The rule governing employee terminations cannot
> apply to promotions for several reasons.
>
> First . . . .
>
> Second . . . .
>
> Third . . . .
>
> Fourth . . . .

Because the topic sentence concept is so critical to a
readable brief, here are illustrations from actual briefs.

Example 1:

> Defendants have moved to disqualify Judge Simon un-
> der 28 USC 455(a), claiming there is a reasonable
> question of his impartiality . . . .
>
> The statute provides:
>
> *   *   *
>
> The test under this section is an objective one . . . .
>
> The court should not disqualify itself unless the
> movants make the requisite showing . . . .

The factual basis forming the disqualification claim must be based on extrajudicial matters and not upon in-court rulings or upon information learned from the court proceeding . . . .

The extrajudicial limitation has resulted in a denial of disqualification in a variety of contexts relevant here . . . .

Defendants have failed to meet these tests for disqualification . . . .

Defendants cite only three decisions in their brief, none of which help them . . . .

Example 2:

The covenant not to compete prohibits the defendants from "soliciting directly or indirectly plaintiff's customers in any form for any reason." . . .

Whether the restraint in the covenant is general or partial makes no difference, for both are condemned under the controlling statute in Michigan . . . .

The statute reflects the basic common law rule that naked restraints of trade are unlawful but ancillary restraints may be upheld in certain circumstances . . . .

Here we have nothing more than a naked restraint, the kind that no Michigan decision has upheld . . . .

Assuming arguendo the covenant is that of an "employee," the plaintiffs fail . . . .

The dream (and only hope) of every plaintiff is to somehow turn an employment or other relationship into a sale of a business under that more liberal and flexible exception . . . .

This transaction is not a sale of a business within the meaning of the statute . . . .

§ 7.07 BRIDGE SENTENCES

What I call a "bridge sentence" is often helpful at the end of a long section. This acts as a transition to the point you are going to make in the next section or series of sections. It often also summarizes or refers to the point just made.

The bridge should not start the next section. Each section should start with its own forceful statement of the involved principle to be discussed or other appropriate introduction. The bridge should both inform and set a less formal tone for the brief.

Examples of bridges after the fact or introductory sections include:

With these facts, we now review the law.

———————————

A preliminary injunction will issue only when plaintiffs demonstrate a likelihood of success on the merits and irreparable harm absent injunctive relief. The following discussion demonstrates plaintiff meets neither burden.

———————————

Before we turn to the asserted grounds of the motion, we consider the grievous misstatements of fact in defendants' moving papers which, by themselves, demonstrate that the matter is not presently ripe for any summary disposition in favor of defendants.

Examples of other bridges include:

We now discuss the two critical prongs of *Howey* [the test for when a transaction involves a security], namely, investment in a "common enterprise" in which profits are "solely from the efforts of the promoter or a third party."

With little legislative history and Supreme Court authority, the canon of construction adopted by the sixth circuit and the application of that canon in the sixth circuit cases assume even greater importance. We turn to this now.

(The last bridge was used as part of an effort to deflect less favorable opinions in sister circuits.)

§ 7.08 QUOTATIONS

Quotations are often essential in a brief. Very often the excerpted quotation is too long. A writer frequently believes the reader will focus on the quotation. Yet if it is too long, the reader may instead skim the quote and concentrate on the text of the brief.

Sometimes a lawyer underscores the essence of the quotation. That is usually a clue that the rest of the quote is unnecessary.

People are more likely to read a short quotation than a long one. Shorten and edit the quotations you use. The extra effort is worthwhile. Here are some pointers.

My preference, when possible, is to extract the key words and not block the quotation at all.

Examples:

Abuse of process requires an ulterior purpose and an act using the process "not proper in the regular conduct or prosecution of the proceedings." The action is the improper "use" of process. [citation]

The commerce requirement is satisfied for a local restraint only if it "substantially and adversely affects interstate commerce."

When you block a quotation, edit generously. Legalese, repetition, and other surplusage permeate many statutes, regulations, and black letter law in opinions. You can always make the full text available in a footnote or appendix.

Eliminate case citations in a blocked quote and simply say "[citations omitted]." If the omitted citation is well known or discussed in your brief, say something like "[citing *Miranda*]."

Sometimes it is better to summarize without quoting. This is true of some archaic statutes. It also applies to lengthy and flowery U.S. Supreme Court statements.

A quotation may stand alone without a lead-in. This is true even at the beginning of a paragraph. For example, you may begin a paragraph:

"The search for Congressional intent begins with the language of the statute." [citation]

Example within a paragraph:

The rule is . . . . [citation] *There the court said:* [quotation].

You may eliminate the italicized words in the last example as long as the jump page before, or the citation after, indicates you are quoting from the case just cited.

Several styles can be used to collect quotes. You may want to collect several quotes, for example, for a judicial gloss on a legal standard. Be succinct. Remember, you don't always need a lead-in. A short series of introductions may organize several blocked quotes.

Example:

The basic principle is not new.

[quotation]

One rationale is this.

[quotation]

The general rule is

[quotation]

When the quotes have essential but primarily back-up value, insert them in parentheses after a citation. This tells the reader he can skim them and not miss your point.

Here is an excerpt from a brief that illustrates some of these pointers:

[1] Federal preemption stems from the supremacy clause of the U.S Constitution, which states all laws of the United States shall be ". . . the Supreme law of the land." [citation]

[2] The U.S. Supreme Court has stated that preemption can occur in three ways:

1. A dominant federal interest or pervasive scheme of federal regulation;

2. An actual conflict between federal and state law;

3. A Congressional expression of unequivocal intent to preempt state law.

[citations]

The Supreme Court has developed several important canons of interpretation.

[3] First, there is always a presumption against preemption.

> Preemption of state law by federal statute or regulation is not favored "in the absence of persuasive reasons — either that the nature of the regulated subject matter permits no other conclusion or that the Congress has unmistakenly so ordained."

[citations]

[4] Second, this presumption is particularly strong in an area "traditionally occupied by the states." [citation] In such a case, "we start with the assumption that the historic police powers of the States were not to be superseded by the Federal Act unless that was the clear and manifest purpose of Congress." [citations] To find a "complete ouster of state power," [citation] there must be "an unambiguous Congressional mandate to that effect." [citation]

[5] Real property law is traditionally the domain of state law. [citations, each followed by a quote in parentheses from the opinion]

Note the following in the previous example: Style [1] excerpts the key relevant words of the supremacy clause. Style [2] summarizes the kinds of preemption. The Supreme Court texts on point are too verbose for a short quote. Although some lower court decisions may lend themselves to a short quote, using one would be inappropriate when the Supreme Court has spoken so often. Style [3] is a short blocked quote. Style [4] is a collection of quotes. Style [5] contains several quotations within the citation portion to emphasize the validity of the summary in the paragraph's topic sentence.

§ 7.09 CITATIONS

Nothing exposes the second-rate lawyer more quickly than an obvious error in citation form. Although you should regularly consult citation authorities, you must master certain elementary principles. The following guidelines should help you with 90 per cent of your citations.

The leading authority on citation form is the Harvard "blue book," A Uniform System of Citation (14th ed). Law reviews require total compliance. The suggestions here eliminate some aspects that seem unnecessary under a plain English theme. Examples of blue book items deleted here are periods in most instances, section signs where it is obvious the reference is to a section, and the year of publication of the current version of a treatise or statute. The suggestions also simplify some items from the blue book, such as later references to cases previously cited in full and references to federal courts of appeal. Whether you follow the Harvard style, these guidelines, or a mixture, be consistent in your style.

Case names are perhaps the most commonly cited authority. Consider this example:

Owen Simon, et al vs *ABC Manufacturing Corporation, et al,* (DC Pa 1974), 474 Fed Supp 963, 967, *aff'd,* 621 Fed 2nd 923 (3d Cir 1975).

Every attorney should recognize many errors here that illustrate fundamental points:

1. Do not use first names of individuals.

2. Do not use "et al"; cite only the first party on a side as if that were the only party

3. Use "v" and not "vs"

4. Use the full technical name of a corporation. Abbreviate the end of the name as "Corp." or "Co" or "Inc." Never say "Co, Inc.," just use "Co." I recommend that you also use abbreviations, for example, "Mfg."

5. Use the name as it appears at the beginning of the case, not as it appears at the top of a later page.

6. The court and year appear at the end. For federal district courts there is no "D.C." If the state has one district, it is simply "D." Otherwise, it will be either ED, WD, SD, ND, or occasionally MD or CD. Do not cite a division. Skip a space only to separate an abbreviation that consists of a capital and lower case letter. For example, ED Pa; SDNY.

7. Similarly, skip a space between the reporter and the series only when the last abbreviation in the report consists of a capital and lower case letter. For example, F2d, ALR4th, but L Ed 2d. "Fed Supp" is

"F Supp," and "Fed 2nd" is "F2d." The "967" in the example is, of course, a jump page to a particular point.

8. The Harvard book is still fighting a rearguard action to cite federal courts of appeal as, for example, "9th Cir." Many people, including many Supreme Court justices, prefer "CA 9."

The case name example then should be

Simon v *ABC Mfg Corp,* 474 F Supp 963, 967 (ED Pa 1974), *aff'd,* 621 F2d 923 (CA 3 1975).

For a state court regional reporter you must cite the state and also the court, if it is not the highest court. If you parallel cite a state court reporter, however, you need not cite the state separately, and you need not cite the court if the state reporter is only for that court or if it is the highest court.

Examples:

Simon v *Rose,* 57 NW2d 321 (Mich Ct App 1977)

Simon v *Rose,* 306 Mich 542, 74 NW2d 101 (1979)

Parallel case citations are not necessary, especially in trial court briefs, for state court opinions. However, you should always use the citation that is the most popular and the most available. For example, cite to the official state reporter in your home state and the regional reporter for other states. Convention requires citing to the official reports of the U.S. Supreme Court, which judges usually have, rather than a private service, which lawyers usually have. Do not cite to a specialty service when the opinion also appears in a general reporter, such as F Supp or FRD. And when you cite to a specialty service or unpublished opinion, send a copy to the judge.

Subsequent references to a case should be brief. When a quotation or other specific reference follows shortly after the full cite, use a jump page in the full cite, and no later cite. If the reference is to the immediately preceding authority, use "*Id.* at [page number]." Examples of alternative forms for later citations include:

Simon, 474 F Supp at 970

474 F Supp at 970

Later case references in the text should also be brief. Say, "the *Simon* court" or "the court in *Simon.*" Do not say, "In *Simon* v *ABC Mfg Corp, supra*" or "In *Simon, supra.*"

The following examples illustrate techniques for some primary sources other than cases.

U.S. Const. amend XIV, §2

Sherman Act §1, 15 USC 1

15 CFR 200.23

Fed R Civ P 12 or FRCP 12

Note the following suggestions:

1. Delete "§" where it follows a compilation reference of statutes or rules.

2. Always cite to the compilation, such as USC and CFR, even if you give the section of the act. The judge almost always uses the compilation.

3. Eliminate the year of compilation for matters currently in force.

4. Designations for the Federal Rules of Civil Procedure can be simply FRCP, as long as in context it is clear the reference is not to the criminal rules.

The following examples illustrate techniques for some secondary sources:

12 CJS, Contracts §220 at 123.

96 ALR3d 424, §3

Restatement (Second) of Torts §501 or Restatement of Torts 2d §501

Prosser, Torts (4th ed) §62

Note the following:

1. The suggestions in this manual eliminate all years of publication but include a reference to the edition of a one-volume or multivolume treatise when this will aid the reader in finding the correct book.

2. In a treatise divided in sections, a number without identification is a page number and with a § signal is a section number.

3. The examples also eliminate the initial of an author's first name.

4. The designation "Annot" is deleted from the ALR cite. Everything in ALR except the lead case opinion is an annotation.

My views on the capitalization of names of statutes are set forth in Section 2.04 of this manual.

§ 7.10 STRING CITATIONS

A string citation is multiple authorities for the same point, usually cited without analysis. Multiple, for our purposes, is more than three. A string citation is appropriate in only limited situations. String citations are least favored for stating well-established principles. Examples: the standard governing summary judgments, preliminary injunctions, or leave to amend. In these instances it is sufficient to cite the leading case and perhaps one other if it better states the test. A purist will also cite an application of the test reaching the result you seek and perhaps a citation to a decision of the court where your case is pending.

You should analyze several cases applying the test only when the application of the test is murky and when you are going to make an analogy from them to your facts. String citations are most important when authority is split on the issue and both sides command support.

§ 7.11 FOOTNOTES

Use footnotes sparingly. The first reason is practical. When the footnote is on the same page as the text, revisions may create mechanical problems with pagination, except for advanced typewriting and word-processing equipment. When they are collected at the end, no one reads them. The second reason is readability. If you expect the material to be read, it flows easier in the main text. A footnote is an interruption.

Many footnotes should be eliminated. Often they involve material the writer recognizes does not belong but cannot bear to cut because it demonstrates the writer's brilliant insight or prodigious research. Such footnotes are required in law review articles, but your brief is not (or should not be) a law review article.

Footnotes are important in several situations. One is extra relevant material you do not necessarily expect a judge to read but want him to have. An example is a full quotation when the brief just has excerpts. (Longer quotations belong in an appendix rather than a footnote.) Another is further caselaw or legislative materials of a marginal nature.

Another situation is to address a point not included in the text of the brief. For example, the brief may concern a preliminary procedural matter, but you are afraid the judge may not initially believe that your underlying claim has merit. This may adversely affect a discretionary ruling. You might add a footnote, such as "Although the merits are not before the court on this motion . . . ." Another example is a response to an opponent's point that you want to deemphasize visually, as well as on the merits, or an explanation of why it is unnecessary to consider a point.

Example:

> Defendants also rely on a regulation. But since the language is identical to the statute, we do not address it separately.

A glossary type footnote is sometimes appropriate at the beginning to explain abbreviated references to the record.

§ 7.12 CONCLUSION

By the time you reach the conclusion you should have already said everything that needs saying. The conclusion is a formality. You should not summarize the grounds for your position except in a very long brief. Always state precisely the relief you seek. The following are examples of the basic format:

> For these reasons, defendants request that the court grant defendants' motion for summary judgment and dismiss the complaint.

> For the reasons stated here and in our main brief, plaintiff requests that the court issue a preliminary injunction in the form requested in the complaint and the motion.

§ 7.13 APPENDIX

The appendix should not include factual material that is not in the record. A brief is simply argument. Attaching documents does not make them part of the record. A brief does not properly authenticate them.

Include documents from the record or deposition excerpts only if they are vital to your position. Do not remake the record. Do not attach documents that are exhibits to an affidavit filed as part of your motion papers. If a short document (such as a letter) is critical, you could, alternatively, reproduce it in the text of the brief. After a statement such as, "[T]his is the letter," leave the rest of the page blank, reproduce the letter on the next numbered page, and resume the text of the brief on the following page.

Legal materials are sometimes proper in an appendix. A long statutory provision excerpted in the text is one example. Photocopy the original. That way neither you nor the reader has to proofread it for accuracy. Another example is agency or legislative material not readily available to the court. A third example is a case on which you heavily rely that is not available in either the court's chambers or the court's central library, such as cases in some CCH services or slip opinions.

§ 7.14 RESPONSIVE BRIEFS

The responsive brief, as noted earlier, usually should state the theory of the main brief for any point the responsive brief attacks. This appears at the beginning of the section. Do not give it too much space — just enough to let the judge look to the responsive brief alone for the complete picture. The body of the section should usually start with your affirmative points, distinguishing the main brief's authorities at the end of the section.

Examples:

> Defendants claim the benefit of the rule that a person acting as an "agent" for both sides in a transaction and accepting a fee from both sides, cannot sue to recover that fee unless he made a prior disclosure of both fees . . . .
>
> The purpose of the rule is the salutory one that an agent owes a fiduciary duty to his principal . . . .
>
> An agency relationship has three essential characteristics . . . .
>
> The record and all available inferences negate an "agency" between plaintiff and defendants . . . .
>
> Defendants have also not established a lack of disclosure for summary judgment purposes . . . .
>
> Defendants' two cases are not on point . . . .

Another important technique is to deflect any excessive rhetoric that, if not addressed, may have a psychological impact on the court.

Examples:

> We learn from the first paragraph of Simon's brief that Rose's papers ignore "fundamental antitrust principles" and, moreover
>
> > . . . contain such glaring omissions of fact and law as to call into question whether Rose seriously recognizes that it is defending against a charge of Sherman Act violation.
>
> This is pretty strong rhetoric. We eagerly and carefully read Simon's 42-page brief and affidavits for an exposition of the fundamental Sherman Act principles

and glaring omissions. Needless to say, we discovered much rhetoric, name-calling, some quotations about the benefits of competition, and some authorities that deal with restraints that have nothing whatever to do with this action. We found nothing that detracted from the analysis of Rose's papers. To the contrary, Simon carefully avoids even mentioning the major thrust of Rose's papers.

Defendant's brief contains broad general conclusions such as the "preemptive effect . . . is firmly established in the case law," a "comprehensive network of agency regulations," "pervasive nature of the regulations," and the agency's "specifically stated intent." Def brief 4. The support and analysis for these grandiose phrases and broad-brush conclusions consist simply of three agency source materials, plus an extensive reliance on one district court opinion, *Simon*. We now show these authorities do not support these statements.

§ 7.15 REPLY BRIEF

The reply brief presents a unique opportunity to present the guts of the matter, in bottom line conclusions, in a context most likely to get the judge's attention. Make the most of it.

The judge may read the reply brief first. It is usually the shortest by far. It is last and may provide shortcuts or roadmaps to the prior briefs. It has the best potential for a quick explanation of the matter. Remember, this is not fiction in which peeking at the end ruins the punchline. This is conveying ideas, persuasively, in which the punchline is critical.

The reply brief has several goals. The most obvious is the standard responsive function of distinguishing points and authorities, noting errors and omissions, and so forth. Equally important, it may quickly summarize your position and show where your opponent failed to address your arguments or issues.

Examples:

Defendants' main brief synthesized the Supreme Court cases on what constitutes a "contract, combination . . . or conspiracy" sufficient to invoke the Sherman Act to test a manufacturer's announced resale restriction policy. The essence is that a combination exists when adherence is secured "by means which go beyond his mere declination to sell to a customer who will not observe his announced policy." Def Brief 25. To avoid a finding of combination, the facts would have to be of "such Doric simplicity as to be somewhat rare in this date of complex business enterprises" *Id.* at 25. Defendants also reviewed the facts that went beyond the "mere announcement" limitation. They were the Simon mass mailing to its customers, the warning about criminal prosecution on the label, soliciting aid from noncustomer retail outlets who acquire the product, and direct interference with direct-buying retail outlets.

Simon's response is a 20-page barrage of quotes and citations that often stand for no more than either the truism that Section 1 requires a finding of "contract, combination . . . or conspiracy" or that none was present on the facts of that reported case. Generally, these quotes have little to do with the issues here. Simon itself cautioned that a decision cannot be divorced from its facts. Simon Brief 41.

For example, several of Simon's precedents do not involve a resale restriction. * * *

Other cases cited by Simon involve a claim of resale restriction, but no proof of any. * * *

Simon, of course, has a firm resale policy applicable to its distribution system and, therefore, we now turn to the very few decisions it cites involving such policies. * * *

Our main brief cited many authorities in support of the crux of this motion — an exclusive lease arrangement of real property is per se lawful. The *Simon* decision is unequivocal. The restriction here is solely on the landowner.

Plaintiff's brief focuses great attention on supposed anticompetitive purposes and effects of the lease restriction. These statements do not advance the inquiry. Here we have an exclusive leasing agreement. That kind of restriction is lawful regardless of damage, regardless of any anticompetitive effects.

§ 7.16 SUPPLEMENTAL LETTER BREIFS

A letter to the judge is an appropriate way to advise him of a new decision, statute, or other authority relevant to a matter under advisement. It should be short and should address only the new material. After all, the issue was fully addressed in the briefs and argument. If the new material is in a slip opinion, specialty service, or other source not regularly available to the judge, enclose a copy.

Example:

Hon. _____

_____

   Re: Simon v Rose

      Civil No _____

Dear Judge _____:

   A recent decision of the Florida Supreme Court confirms defendant's position on the pending summary judgment motion. [citation] A copy is enclosed. There,
. . .

Lawyers sometimes manufacture excuses to write a letter when the judge has the matter under advisement an unduly long time. Perhaps the judge will advance the matter from the bottom of his pile. You might gently say the following.

Dear Judge _____:

   The summary judgment motion was argued on _____. Recently, the ninth circuit held . . . .

Always send these letters to all counsel, even if the letters are not technically papers "filed" with the court.

8

Discovery

§ 8.01 INTRODUCTION

There are more individual styles among attorneys for basic written discovery requests — interrogatories, document requests, and requests for admissions — than for virtually any other paper reviewed in this manual. The style of any individual attorney may vary, depending on the complexity of the action. You should also carefully consider what you want to accomplish in the request. Do you want to narrow issues, preserve evidence, pin the witness down, exhaust proofs, and so forth? The modest goal of this chapter is to state a few rules of required form, present some style pointers, and suggest a few strategy tips.

A comprehensive form book is helpful at times in discovery matters, as a checklist for assuring that you have sought all of the kinds of information needed for the particular kind of case.

§ 8.02 DEPOSITION NOTICE

The formal requirements of a deposition notice are few. The notice must state the time and place of the deposition and the name and address of the deponent, or a general description sufficient to identify the deponent if the name is unknown. FRCP 30(b)(1). (Notices frequently omit the address of the deponent, even though it is required. This manual does also.) The notice to a party may direct the deponent to produce "documents and tangible things" at the deposition. FRCP 30(b)(5).

The deposition of a nonparty is compelled only through a subpoena, FRCP 45, a form usually obtained from the court. The subpoena issues after a deposition notice to the parties is served. FRCP 45(d)(1). The deposition notice must attach any document request included in the subpoena. FRCP 30(b)(1).

Some information often included in a notice is unnecessary. You need not state that the deposition will be conducted according to the court rules. Obviously it must be. You need not state that the deposition will be taken before a notary public. The rules identify the persons before whom a deposition is taken. FRCP 28. Nor need you state that other attorneys are invited to attend and cross-examine. This right is expressly granted in the rules. FRCP 30(c). Litigants are presumed to know the rules. If they do not, it is not your problem.

Suggested notice:

DEPOSITION NOTICE

Plaintiff will take the deposition of defendant Owen Simon on ——————, 198— at ————————————— [AM or PM] at [e.g., the office of Smith & Jones] located at ———————————————————————. Deponent is requested to bring to the deposition the documents identified on the exhibit to this notice.

Suggested notice for several depositions:

DEPOSITION NOTICE

Plaintiff will take the following depositions, in the order named, on ——————, 198— at ———————— ———————— [AM or PM] at ———————————:

1. Defendant Owen Simon

2. Defendant Susan Rose

The depositions will continue from day to day until completed.

[Document request language]

Note the following:

1. A notice of several depositions in a row, without specific starting times, is common. It may be subject to attack, however, if the noticing party is unable to work out an arrangement so that deponents do not wait a long time for their depositions.

2. The form can be readily modified to provide for times certain. The preamble should say "on the dates and times listed below," and this information should appear after the deponent's names.

3. The "day to day" language is appropriate when the depositions may last more than one day. This applies even to the notice of a single deposition.

When the deponent is a "managing agent" of a corporate party, I suggest this style for naming the deponent:

> . . . the deposition of defendant XYZ Corp by its director, president, and managing agent, Owen Simon, and the deposition of [defendant] Owen Simon individually.

Two reasons support this style of noticing the entity's deposition. First, when the deponent is a managing agent, the deposition can proceed by notice without a subpoena. The deponent is the entity party. Second, any discovery sanctions will be imposed on the party, not just the individual. Both concepts are probably implicit even if the notice just names the individual. This style, however, makes your position explicit and unambiguous. In the example, "managing agent" is technically sufficient and you may delete "director, president." If the person is not an individual defendant, noticing the deposition "individually" may be arguably improper without a subpoena. I include it anyway.

The approach to a corporate managing agent subpoena may be adapted for partnerships and other entity parties.

When you don't know the name of a person, a description identifying that person is permitted. Many attorneys notice a deposition by description even if they think an identified person is the one described. When a named managing agent of a nonparty corporation is avoiding subpoena service, a description subpoena may be served on the corporation. A description notice avoids problems when a named deponent claims that someone else has knowledge.

Examples:

Keeper of the records of XYZ Corp.

Day-shift nurse in charge of the third floor of City Hospital.

A deposition notice to a corporation, government agency, partnership, or association may merely identify with "reasonable particularity" the matters for examination. The organization must then designate a person to testify and identify the matters on which he will testify. FRCP 30(b)(6). A subpoena to a nonparty under this subrule must advise of the duty to make a designation.

Examples:

. . . the deposition of XYZ Corp on the matter of its minority hiring and promotion policy by its Rule 30(b)(6) designee.

. . . the deposition of the Securities Exchange Commission by its Rule 30(b)(6) representative who has knowledge of the factual basis of its audit report of defendant.

The form for a document request on the exhibit to a deposition notice is the same as the form for nondeposition document requests discussed in Section 8.04. Use an independent document request in addition to the one in the deposition notice when you believe the deposition may be adjourned. The time period for the independent request keeps running unless it, too, is separately extended by a stipulation or order.

§ 8.03 INTERROGATORIES

The formal requirements in the rules for interrogatories to another party are minimal. They may relate to facts, an opinion or contention that relates to fact, or to the application of law to fact. FRCP 33(b). If you have difficulty determining in which category a request fits, don't worry. That very difficulty is what led to the expansion beyond pure facts in the present rule formulation. However, questions may not relate to pure legal issues apart from facts involved in the action.

The party to whom interrogatories are addressed may answer, object, produce business records as the answer in certain circumstances, seek to defer the answer, or, as in any discovery matter, seek a protective order. FRCP 33 and 26(c). Answers must be stated "separately and fully" and must include "such information as is available to the party." FRCP 33(a). Available information includes information known to employees, agents, and similar persons. In other words, the answer must be based on a reasonable investigation. Objections must include the reason for the objection. *Id.*

The party must sign answers "under oath" and, under recent changes, the attorney must also sign answers with the implicit certification the signature represents. FRCP 11 and 26(g). The effect of this amendment is that sanctions may now be imposed on the attorney. *Id.* If the attorney does not sign, move to strike the response, as permitted by the rules.

You may, but need not, include matters that are expressly covered in the rules, such as the time period for the response, the duty to make a reasonable investigation, or the duty to supplement responses in certain instances.

Organize interrogatories in a logical and easy-to-follow sequence. An appropriate order may be to group the requests in the general order of pleadings: (1) parties and background, (2) substantive claim, (3)relief, and (4) special defenses. Big cases often have these categories in separate sets of interrogatories.

The subject matter of the questions may track the complaint as in this example:

7. State each fact on which you rely to support your claim of duress in paragraph 12 of the complaint.

8. Define specifically what is meant by "reasonable expectations" in paragraph 13 of the complaint.

9. State the amount of income you believe you lost because of the misrepresentation listed in paragraph 14 of the complaint and describe how you arrived at the amount or estimate.

Analytically separate a string of elements into separate questions. For example, a complaint may allege that the defendant had contractual, fiduciary, and other duties. Ask about each separately, even if you believe the answer will be the same to all.

Interrogatories often begin, after the short introduction, with a lengthy standard form set of definitions and instructions. Within a question use these broad definitions unless a more restrictive word is required by the question. For example, if you broadly define "document" in the introduction, ask for documents, not memos or letters.

The following is an example of introduction, definitions, and instructions:

DEFENDANT'S INTERROGATORIES TO PLAINTIFFS — SET NO. 1

Defendant submits these interrogatories to plaintiffs pursuant to FRCP 33.

Definitions

The following terms have the following meanings in these interrogatories:

1. "Person" includes any individual, corporation, partnership, group, association, governmental entity, or any other organization.

2. "You" or "your" and "plaintiffs" refer to plaintiffs and their subsidiaries and any merged or acquired predecessors, past and present officers, employees, agents, and all other persons acting or purporting to act on behalf of plaintiffs or such subsidiaries or predecessors.

3. "Document" means any written, printed, typed, or other graphic or photographic matter of any nature and any audio or video recordings in your possession, custody, or control, or known by you to exist or to have existed. All copies of documents that contain any alter-

ations or annotations or that differ in any other way from the originals or copies referred to in the preceding sentence are deemed separate documents from the originals or copies.

4. "Communicate" or "communication" means every manner of disclosure or exchange, and every disclosure or exchange, of information, whether orally or by document or whether face-to-face, by telephone, mail, personal delivery, or otherwise.

5. "Identify" used in reference to an individual person means to state (a) the person's full name and present or last known address, (b) the person's present or last known position and business affiliation, and (c) the person's position and business affiliation at the time in question. "Identify" used in reference to any other person means to state (a) the person's full name and present or last known address, (b) type of entity and (c) the names of the individual persons who are or were principals, agents, or employees and who have knowledge of relevant facts.

6. "Identify" used in reference to a document means to state (a) the date, (b) author or addressor, (c) addressee and recipients of all copies, (d) type of document (for example, letter, memorandum, telegram, chart, photograph, brochure) or some other means of identifying it, and (e) its present location or custodian. If any document was but no longer is in your possession or subject to your control, state what disposition was made of it and the identity of the person you reasonably believe to be the present custodian. Instead of the identification, you may furnish the documents for inspection and copying at the time you serve answers to these interrogatories.

7. "Identify" used in reference to a communication means to state (a) its date, (b) the place where it oc-

curred, (c) the type of communication (for example, telephone conversation, meeting), (d) its substance, (e) the identity of the person who made it, (f) the identity of each person who received it and of all other persons who were present.

Instructions

1. For every interrogatory that requests you to state the basis of an allegation [substitute "denial" if a plaintiff], answer as follows:

(a) Describe in detail the complete factual basis for the allegation;

(b) Identify every communication that relates to the allegation;

(c) Identify every document that relates to the allegation;

(d) Identify every person who has knowledge of facts relating to the allegation;

2. Unless otherwise indicated, these interrogatories cover the period from _____ to _____.

3. With respect to any document or communication for which you claim a privilege, identify the document or communication as required above, including the general subject matter, but not the substance, state the privilege involved, and state the factual and legal basis of the privilege . . . .

Interrogatories

1. . . .

These definitions and instructions are used to make the questions themselves briefer. Example, using the definitions:

With respect to your allegation that plaintiff signed the agreement under duress:

(a) identify all persons with knowledge of any relevant facts;

(b) identify all communications that relate to the allegation;

(c) identify all documents that relate to the allegation;

(d) state all other facts that support the allegation.

Example, using the instructions to get the same information:

State the basis for the allegation that plaintiff signed the agreement under duress.

Some lawyers attempt to extend this style to its extreme.

Examples:

State the basis for your claim in Count I.

Identify all communications relating to the allegations of the complaint and answer.

Identify all documents relating to the allegations of the complaint and answer.

Identify all persons with knowledge of the allegations of the complaint and answer and state the basis of their knowledge.

A strong word of caution is in order. There comes a point, depending on the complexity of the action and the philosophy of the judge, when interrogatories are objectionable because they are burdensome, not reasonably specific, or for other reasons. Discovery abuse prompted the 1983 amendment to FRCP 26(b)(1), which authorizes limiting discovery that is out of proportion to the action. There is also the risk of deferral of the answer. One philosophy, however, is to ask for all of this anyway, on the theory that a compromise is available later, that is, you can always back off.

If you ask broad questions, always have more specific questions as well for the information you really need. You may then, perhaps, begin the broad interrogatory with something like: "To the extent not set forth in your answers to other interrogatories, identify . . . ." Since it is a matter of degree, the narrower your question, the greater the chance it will survive objection or deferral. You don't want the information you really need to be delayed by objections to other overbroad aspects of your questions.

Many attorneys preparing answers simply disregard some burdensome parts of information requested in the "identification" definitions. The theory is that the proponent will not pursue the matter or, at worst, the answer will have to be supplemented. Examples from the definitions are the address of a person identified in the answer or identity of the recipients of copies of a document.

The form of questions seeking information about persons and documents generates many disputes. Interrogatories often ask for a list of trial witnesses, trial exhibits, or evidence the opponent plans to introduce. Some authorities suggest that a party should not be forced to reveal this trial strategy until the final pretrial conference, or just before trial. On the other hand, properly phrased questions seeking (a) the name and location of persons with knowledge of the facts or (b) the existence, description, and location of relevant documents, or (c) a list of other relevant matters on which the party relies are in the hard core of permitted discovery. *See* FRCP 26(b)(1).

Another standard interrogatory for learning who has what relevant knowledge is to inquire about the persons who prepared the answers for an entity.

Example:

> Identify the person signing these interrogatory answers on your behalf.
>
> Identify each person who provided information for your answers and, for each person, list the interrogatory numbers involved.

Although interrogatories may not seek documents, you may combine them in one paper with a document request under the document request rule. Indicate the dual nature in the document title, and include the dual nature in the introductory language. One of several approaches is to add a numbered paragraph, such as this, in the body of the paper.

> Plaintiff requests defendant to produce all documents identified in the answers to these interrogatories.

Alternatively, you may make specific requests throughout the document.

I turn now to the style of responses.

Objections and answers may be combined in one document. Under prior practice, only the party signed answers; the attorney signed objections. Many lawyers filed separate documents. Although this is unnecessary now that lawyers must sign answers, it is still acceptable. Several parties may jointly file answers in one document, as long as no confusion is created about who is swearing to which answers or who has what knowledge.

You may incorporate other interrogatory answers as all or part of an interrogatory answer.

Example:

See answer to 10(b)

Lengthy sets of interrogatories, with overlapping questions, frequently create many opportunities for incorporation.

Do not incorporate material outside the interrogatory answers, especially when the reader must make an elaborate comparison. Several decisions, for example, frown on incorporating rambling discourses in depositions.

You may incorporate an identical objection without restating it fully.

Example:

See objection to 10(c).

It is improper to simply decline to answer a proper question merely because you will not have the information until you take discovery. You have two choices in this instance. Either seek to have the answer deferred until a later time, FRCP 33(b), or answer, based on your present knowledge, that you have no responsive information. If you do not get an order of deferral, the proponent is entitled to know that you have no present facts. A likely subject for deferral is plaintiff's damages.

The option to produce business records as the answer to the interrogatory applies when the answer may be found in the records and the burden of finding the answer is the same for either party. FRCP 33(c). The rules require you to specify the records in sufficient detail to permit the proponent to locate them. In practice, lawyers often do not list specific records in the answer but simply produce the specific records involved.

Example:

> Defendant will produce its business records pursuant to FRCP 33(c).

Objections must include the reasons for objecting. Don't write a legal analysis. Just identify the reasons.

Example:

> Defendant objects to this interrogatory because it is outside the scope of discovery set forth in FRCF 26(b)(1).

When the reason is a privilege, such as the attorney-client privilege, you must provide sufficient information to permit the court to determine whether the privilege is properly invoked.

§ 8.04 DOCUMENT REQUESTS

The form of a document request is easy to master. The rules require two things. The request must specify "a reasonable time, place, and manner of making the inspection . . ." The request must set forth the items for inspection by individual item or category, each of which must be described "with reasonable particularity." FRCP 34(b).

The introductory portion of the request may state a specific time and place for making the production, as FRCP Form 24 suggests, or it may have a more general provision under which the parties will later mutually work out arrangements, as suggested in 8 Wright and Miller, Federal Practice and Procedure §2212 at 636.

Example:

> Defendants request the plaintiff, pursuant to Rule 34, to produce and permit defendants, their attorneys, and agents to inspect and copy the documents listed below at the office of Simon & Rose on _____ [or "at a time and place convenient to plaintiff within _____ _____ days of service of this request"].

Note the following:

1. The introduction need not remind the other party to serve a written response to the request. It is required by the rules. It may be useful, however, since many attorneys do not know they must serve a written response.

2. The phrase "their attorneys and agents" is not strictly necessary, since the rules expressly permit

someone acting on behalf of the party making the request to inspect and copy the documents.

3. You need not remind the other party that he must produce all documents in his possession, custody, or control, since this also is expressly required by the rules.

4. When the introduction has a date certain and you know the production will be voluminous, you may add that the inspection will continue "from day to day until completed."

Most requests also define "document" even though the rules contain a definition. FRCP 34(a). Attorneys typically have a standard definition they always use, and for this reason it is often overly inclusive. Much like the lengthy laundry list of matters in releases (for example, claims, demands), these definitions can be shorter without any loss of substance.

Document requests sometimes contain other definitions, such as "plaintiffs," and instructions, such as the time period and information to include in claiming privilege in the response.

The following is an example of definitions (using part of the definition in the rules) and instructions:

Definitions and Instructions

1. "Document" means any written, printed, typed, or other graphic or photographic matter of any nature, any audio or video recordings, and other data compilations from which information can be obtained, translated, if necessary, by you through detection devices into reasonably usable form. All copies of documents

that contain any alterations, annotations, or that differ in any other way from the originals or copies referred to in the preceding sentence are deemed separate documents from the originals or copies.

2. Unless otherwise indicated, these requests for documents cover the period from _____ _____ through _____.

3. With respect to any document for which you claim a privilege, identify the document, state the privilege involved, and state the factual and legal basis for the claimed privilege. Identify the document by stating (a) the type of document (letter, memo, and so forth), (b) the identity of the author, (c) the date written or originated, (d) the identity of each person to whom the original or a copy was addressed or delivered, and (e) the identity of every other person who has ever had possession of the document.

Organize the requests themselves in a logical sequence as suggested for interrogatories.

Often it is useful to separate a specific key document from the catch-all request. This isolates the key document from the rest and prevents it from being absorbed in a potential objection. The catch-all may be divided also.

Example:

1. The lease between the parties, including all amendments.

2. If the plaintiff does not have a signed copy of the lease or any amendment, then an unsigned counterpart of that document.

3. All documents relating to the negotiation of the lease or any amendments sent by one party to the other party, including, for example, all preliminary drafts.

4. All documents relating to the lease or any amendment, excluding documents relating to rent payments.

Note that the requests become progressively broader.

Requests may be objectionable as overbroad even though they superficially appear to have reasonable particularity. Much depends on the particular judge and on the request in the context of the action. For example, to ask for all documents relating to "your damages" or "your claims in Count II" may be overbroad. On the other hand, all documents defendant has that relate "to plaintiff" or "to plaintiff's customers" in a trade secret action may be appropriate. It is a matter of degree. One aspect of the test is that a reasonable person should be able to determine what documents to assemble. That is another reason for sometimes stating requests progressively from the specific to the general.

The introductory phrase of catch-all requests is often repetitive, for example: "all documents that record, recount, relate in any way to, or are connected with, . . ." Simply say: "all documents relating to . . . ."

A cross-reference to other discovery devices is often useful.

Examples:

All documents identified in any answer to, or the identification of which was requested in, plaintiff's interrogatories.

All documents identified in any responses to plaintiff's request for admissions.

The following is an example of specific responses:

Defendant responds to plaintiff's request for documents as follows:

1. Inspection will be permitted as requested.

2. Inspection will be permitted but not on the date requested because it will take at least two more weeks to assemble the responsive documents.

3. Inspection will be permitted as requested, except defendant objects to the request for federal income tax returns because . . . .

4. This request is objected to because . . . .

Here is a streamlined style for the response to lengthy document requests in courts in which you need not repeat the request:

Defendant will permit the inspection as requested with respect to each item or category except as set forth below.

1. Defendant objects to request 12 because . . . .

§ 8.05 REQUESTS FOR ADMISSION

A request for admissions to another party may relate to (1) statements or opinions of fact, (2) application of law to fact, or (3) the genuineness of documents. FRCP 36(a). Pure matters of law unrelated to fact are not permitted.

Responses are tightly governed by the rules, which provide seven options. FRCP 36(a) and 26(c). (1) A party may object to a request but must state the reason. (2) A party may deny the matter, subject to two requirements: First, a denial must "fairly meet the substance" of the requested admission; second, if "good faith" requires a qualified denial or partial admission, you must do so by specifying what is true and qualifying or denying the rest. (3) A party may decline to admit or deny based on a lack of information or knowledge only if the response states that he made reasonable inquiry and the information known or readily obtainable is insufficient to respond. (4) A party may deny or state the reasons why he can't respond, subject to the sanctions provision if the response is unreasonable, but the party cannot merely say that there is a genuine issue for trial. (5) A party may seek a protective order under that separate rule. (6) A party may admit the request. (7) If a party makes no timely objection or response, the matter is deemed admitted.

A special provision provides stiff sanctions against a party for failing to admit a matter that is later proved. FRCP 37(c). The court, on motion, shall award reasonable expenses, including attorney fees, unless the request was objectionable or of no importance, the party had "reasonable ground" to believe he might prevail, or there is other "good ground" for failing to admit.

As with interrogatories, under recent rule changes the attorney, as well as the party, must sign the response, so that sanctions are available against the attorney. FRCP 11 and 26(g). Move to strike any response not signed by the attorney.

The philosophy of this discovery tool is important for its effective use. Unlike other discovery devices, the primary purpose of requests for admissions is not to discover facts but to narrow the issues for trial by gaining admissions of matters the proponent already knows. Properly used, and with the sanctions in mind, it can and should narrow areas of dispute and streamline the lawsuit. Almost all lawsuits could benefit from increased use of requests for admissions.

The general rules of form are relatively few. Each matter must be in a separately numbered paragraph. FRCP 36(a). The request should be simple and direct so that it may be admitted or denied with a minimum of qualification or evasion. Generally avoid the use of phrases that can be evaded, such as "unreasonable" or "excessive." Any documents must be furnished with the request unless they are otherwise made available. Do not incorporate by reference; the request and response alone should define the status of the admission. An exception may be to refer to a document that is an exhibit to a complaint or other court paper.

The response to all requests must be in one document, whether it is an objection, admission, denial, or other response. The paragraph numbers of the response must coincide with those of the request.

The following is an example of request and response style in an employment termination action:

REQUEST FOR ADMISSIONS

Plaintiff requests defendant to make the following admissions pursuant to FRCP 36.

1. Defendant discharged plaintiff on July 23, 1984. [statement of fact]

2. Defendant discharged plaintiff because she complained about sexual advances by her supervisor A. Smith. [statement or opinion of fact]

3. Defendant could not discharge plaintiff without "good cause." [application of law to fact]

4. An employee for an indefinite term can only be discharged for cause when the company has unilaterally announced such a policy. [pure law unrelated to fact]

5. Exhibit A to plaintiff's affidavit of 7/5/84 is a genuine copy of plaintiff's employment contract with defendant. [genuineness of a document]

6. Plaintiff suffered emotional distress as a result of the discharge.

RESPONSE TO REQUEST FOR ADMISSIONS

Defendant responds to plaintiff's request for admissions as follows:

1. Admit.

2. Denies that defendant discharged plaintiff because she complained about sexual advances by her supervisor A. Smith but admits plaintiff made such complaints. [qualified denial]

3. Deny.

4. Defendant objects to this request because it is outside the scope of discovery. It seeks an admission of a pure statement of law unrelated to the facts of this action. [objection]

5. Admit.

6. Defendant lacks information sufficient to enable it to admit or deny, states it has inquired of plaintiff's current employer and her psychiatrist, and is unable to respond. [lack of knowledge]

6. Defendant cannot admit or deny this request, which is outside of its knowledge until defendant conducts discovery. Defendant believes this request presents a genuine issue for trial because, for example, plaintiff immediately accepted another job without any loss of work [cannot admit or deny]

Use interrogatories to discover the basis for denials of requests for admissions.

§ 8.06 CONFIDENTIALITY ORDERS

Protective orders frequently designate the procedures for disclosure of confidential information. FRCP 26(c). Typically the parties stipulate to the procedures.

Many formats are used. Some orders define what constitutes the confidential information. Others require court involvement before matters are deemed confidential. I prefer self-designation, with the right to go to court later to challenge the designation. This way you get the information before any contested court matter.

The following is the form I have used. Under the philosophy of this manual, it could be streamlined. I leave that to the reader.

PROTECTIVE ORDER

Upon stipulation of the parties, the court enters this protective order under FRCP 26(c). As used in this order, "confidential information" means information a party has designated as confidential.

IT IS ORDERED that, if in the course of this action, any party has occasion to disclose confidential information, the following procedures shall be employed and the following restrictions shall govern:

Written Materials

1. Any document filed in this action, any transcript of deposition, or any documents produced for inspection and copying, when designated by the producing party to contain confidential information, may be exhibited to, or the contents discussed with, or disclosed to, the following persons only: counsel of record, their office associates or office employees, and independent experts not connected in any way with the parties, their directors, officers, or employees. These persons are prohibited from disclosing the documents or discussing their contents with any other person. Each nonattorney permitted by this order to receive information designated as confidential information, before receiving this information, shall be shown a copy of this order and shall agree in writing to be bound by its terms.

Oral Testimony

2. Any testimony upon an oral deposition, when designated by counsel for a party deponent to contain confidential information, shall be separately transcribed and appropriately labeled. Only those persons designated in paragraph 1 may listen to this testimony, and they shall be bound by the restrictions contained in paragraph 1.

Papers Filed in Court

3. Any documents, including briefs, transcripts of testimony, answers to interrogatories, or other papers, subject to the provisions of this order, and any documents making reference to confidential information in these documents, when filed in this court, shall be sealed under an order of the court permitting disclosure only to persons designated in paragraph 1.

Court Review and Modification

4. Any party may bring before the court at any time the question whether any particular document, material, or information does or does not, in fact, contain confidential information.

5. The court may modify this order as the court may find appropriate, and either party may apply to the court at any time for a modification of this order.

Conclusion of Action

6. Upon the final determination of this action, all documents, transcripts of testimony, answers to interrogatories, or other papers subject to the provisions of this order shall be delivered by counsel for the receiving party to counsel for the disclosing party. All copies or summaries, memoranda, and notes reflecting their contents or substance shall be destroyed.

No Admission

7. The designation by a disclosing party of any document or information as constituting or containing confidential information is intended solely to facilitate the preparation and trial of this action. Such a designation is not an admission by any party that the designated disclosure constitutes or contains any confidential information.

9

Miscellaneous Papers

§ 9.01 APPEARANCE

The old style is to address this document to the clerk, like a letter.

Example:

APPEARANCE

To the clerk of the court:

Please enter our appearance for _____.

This is unnecessary. A docket clerk who processes a paper called an appearance knows what to do without the special salutation. Suggested form:

APPEARANCE

The undersigned appears for _____

§ 9.02 STIPULATIONS

Stipulations are fertile ground for excess words. A preamble often looks like this:

STIPULATION

The parties, by and through their undersigned counsel of record, hereby stipulate and agree . . . .

So far, all this says is "the parties agree." The operative language should be plain language and should be as brief as possible. When a stipulation provides for filing a document, simply refer to the document rather than reciting its terms.

Example:

STIPULATION

The parties agree that the court may enter an order in the form attached to this stipulation . . . .

Procedurally, the attachment to the stipulation remains an unsigned copy, as it is a part of the stipulation. The court enters and dockets a separate copy. (Incidentally, the recital in the order may read, "The parties have stipulated that the court may enter this order. It is ordered . . . .")

§ 9.03 EXTENSIONS OF TIME

Papers frequently provide for extensions of time to serve or file a paper or to do something. Usually the parties define the extension as a time period, such as two weeks or 30 days. There is often uncertainty, however, about the original date that is being extended.

For example, the lawyer may not know the date the complaint was served on his client. Extensions are precise if styled as a specific day, rather than as a time period.

Example:

> The time for defendant to serve a response to the complaint is extended to June 6, 1988.

Note that the extension is to "respond" to the complaint, not to "answer." The reason is that the defendant may either answer or file a preanswer motion.

Extensions should be to "serve" a paper rather than to "file" it. Service is complete on mailing. FRCP 5(b). Filing is complete when received by the clerk. FRCP 5(e). The difference is painfully obvious when the paper is completed in late afternoon and the choice is a messenger or the nearest mailbox.

Time periods in the federal rules are for service, with filing permitted within a reasonable time afterward. FRCP 5.

§ 9.04 SUBSTITUTION OF ATTORNEYS

Attorneys often prepare a separate "consent to substitution of attorneys" and a separate "appearance" of the new attorney. You may also provide for a court order. You may combine these in a simple form.

Example:

SUBSTITUTION OF ATTORNEYS

Simon & Rose is substituted as attorneys and appears for defendant.

[signature of original   [signature of
attorneys of record]   Simon & Rose]

SO ORDERED:

_____

District Judge

Another style:

ORDER OF SUBSTITUTION OF ATTORNEYS

It is ordered that Simon & Rose is substituted as attorneys for defendant.

_____

District Judge

Consent to order   Appearance for defendant
[signature of original   [signature of Simon & Rose]
attorneys of record]

You may devise an alternative style, perhaps better than these. Substitution of counsel is an easy place to test your own concise, common-sense approach to style.

§ 9.05 LIS PENDENS

A lis pendens, often written in legalese, may easily be converted to plain English. Under state law this document usually must contain the name of the action, the "general object" of the lawsuit, and a legal description of the affected land.

Example:

[Caption]

NOTICE OF LIS PENDENS

An action was filed and is now pending in the above named court. Defendant is the vendee under a land contract dated _____ and sold its vendee's interest to plaintiffs under a land contract dated _____. Plaintiffs allege mutual mistake and intentional misrepresentation and seek reformation of their land contract with defendant, a declaration of rights, and damages. The land affected by this action is situated in _____ and is described as follows:

[insert legal description]

[attorney signature]

§ 9.06 RELEASE IN SETTLEMENTS

Settlements often include mutual releases. They are perhaps the ultimate example of redundant words. Either lawyers are particularly cautious in drafting releases, or (more likely) they just copy an old form.

The release usually dominates the settlement paper. It should be sufficient for a party to simply release "all claims." Yet most of us are not willing to extend plain language this far; we need a few more words for comfort. My compromise is

Plaintiff _____ and defendant ____ _____ release each other as well as the directors, officers, employees, and agents of the other from all claims against each other they have, or may have, known or unknown, including, but not limited to, the claims in the complaint and counterclaim in *Smith* v *Jones,* Civ No 82-7016, ED Mich.

Note these pointers: The release names each person or entity releasing and each one being released. The release is general, but it specifically identifies the current claim.

A special problem arises when there are several plaintiffs, *A, B,* and *C,* and several defendants, *D, E,* and *F.* Do not say "*A, B, C, D, E,* and *F* release each other . . . ." The effect of this may be that the parties on one side, such as *A, B* and *C,* release each other, although the intent is only for one side to release the other side. One solution:

> *A, B,* and *C,* on the one hand, and *D, E,* and *F,* on the other hand, release each other, as well as . . . .

When the release is one section of a settlement agreement, precede the release section with "Except for rights under this agreement . . . ."

Some attorneys find comfort in this additional thought at the end of the release:

> The parties have signed this agreement freely. No promises were made to obtain the release except for the payment plaintiff has received to settle the complaint previously described.

§ 9.07 CORRESPONDENCE

Correspondence should be less formal and crisper than papers filed in court. Too often it isn't.

The name and address is the most formal part of the letter.

Examples:

Owen Simon, Esq.
Simon & Rose
[address]

Hon. Owen Simon
[Chief Judge]
United States District Court
Eastern District of Michigan
[address]

Hon. Owen Simon
[Chief Judge]
United States Court of Appeals
   for the Sixth Circuit
[address]

Note the following. All attorneys, male or female, are "Esq." Never say "Mr. Owen Simon, Esq." And never say "Attorney at Law" under the name. That is what "Esq." means. Put the name of the law firm under the attorney's name.

The "Re" should be less formal than the official caption for court papers. For example, *Texaco, Inc* v *Corner Gas Station Corp* could be

Re: Texaco v Corner Gas

Do not say:

Re: Owen Simon, et al. v Susan Rose, et al.

Instead, say:

Re: Simon v Rose

When there are multiple actions or cross actions, you can designate them by the chief parties or individuals or by the subject matter.

Examples:

Re: Simon — Rose

Re: Due on sale cases

Re: Continental bankruptcy cases

Domestic relations matters often use this style:

Re: Smith, Owen and Susan

The civil number is only necessary when writing to the court. Some firms put their office file number as part of the "Re."

The text, especially in transmittal letters, can be brief.

Old style:

> In the above-referenced matter, enclosed herein please find Defendant's Memorandum in Opposition to Plaintiff's Motion for Class Certification.

Suggested style:

I enclose our class action brief.

Note: The phrase "in the above-referenced matter" is redundant. The "Re" states the subject of the letter. Nor need you include the technical name of a document.

Letters often record a telephone agreement. Often the writer asks the addressee to confirm in writing, such as by signing a copy of the letter and returning it. Sometimes this is wise. I rarely seek written confirmation from the other side. What if the lawyer does not give it? Is there no agreement? Unilaterally stating the agreement or inviting a reply if the recipient disagrees

leaves the practical burden (whatever the legal nice-
ties) on the recipient to come forward if he differs.

The signature need not have the formality of a document filed in court. An individual signature, not the
firm, is proper (except in law firm opinion letters).
Use:

Sincerely yours,

Owen Simon

Don't use:

Simon & Rose

By: _____

Owen Simon

The complimentary close of letters to judges and other
"high officials" should be "Respectfully yours."

When listing copies or "cc," here are suggested rules.
When sending a copy to a client that is an entity, list
the entity itself as the recipient of the copy. It is not the
addressee's business to know which individual you
send the copy to. Second, do not list interoffice copies.
Third, if the recipients are numerous, use one or more
general designations.

Examples:

   cc: Plaintiffs

   cc: All counsel of record

10

Words

§ 10.01 INTRODUCTION

Several excellent books cover words, sentence structure, and other matters of good legal writing style. These include MELLINKOFF, LEGAL WRITING: SENSE AND NONSENSE; WYDICK, PLAIN ENGLISH FOR LAWYERS; SQUIRES AND ROMBAUER, LEGAL WRITING; BISKIND, SIMPLIFY LEGAL WRITING. This manual, with its specific lawsuit focus, will not repeat the careful analysis of these works, except for some matters covered in the chapter on briefs. However, two of these authors organized good legal writing into "golden rules" that bear repeating.

Wydick advances six principles of plain English:

1. Omit surplus words.
2. Use familiar, concrete words.
3. Use short sentences.
4. Use base verbs and the active voice.

5. Arrange your words with care.

6. Avoid language quirks.

Mellinkoff establishes seven rules:

1. Peculiar — The language of the law is more peculiar than precise. Don't confuse peculiarity with precision.

2. Precise — Don't ignore even the limited possibilities of precision. The price of sloppy writing is misunderstanding and creative misinterpretation.

3. English — Follow the rules of English composition.

4. Clear — Usually you have a choice of how to say it. Choose clarity.

5. Law — Write law simply. Do not puff, mangle, or hide.

6. Plan — Before you write, plan.

7. Cut! — Cut it in half!

§ 10.02 WORDS TO AVOID

You should almost never use archaic words.

Examples:

here group	
hereafter	hereby
herein	hereof
hereinafter	heretofore
hereinbefore	hereunto
	herewith

there group	*others*
thenceforth	cause [lawsuit or action]
therefrom	inasmuch
therein	insofar
thereto	to wit
thereunto	
therewith	*referring back*
	aforesaid
where group	foregoing
whereas	premises [as referring to
whereby	something referred to]
wherein	said [as referring to
whereof	something referred to]
whereon	same [as a noun]

phrases

now comes
further affiant saith not
now, therefore

§ 10.03 REDUNDANT WORDS

You should not couple words with the same common meaning.

Examples:

alter or change	by and through
attorney and counsellor	cease and desist
bind and obligate	covenant and agree

due and owing	modified and changed
each and every	null and void
for and in behalf of	ordered, adjudged,
for and during	and decreed
force and effect	over and above
from and after	part and parcel
full force and effect	sole and exclusive
in truth and in fact,	stipulate and agree
or true fact	suffer or permit
just and reasonable	then and in that event
known and described as	true and correct
made and entered into	understood and agreed

§ 10.04 ACCEPTABLE TECHNICAL WORDS

Lawsuit papers are written for lawyers and judges. Some technical words are appropriate. They may have a well-known meaning or may evoke a specific doctrine. A plain English translation may be cumbersome. The rule may be different for consumer contracts and other papers for laymen. In lawsuits they are proper.

Examples:

amicus curiae	laches
caveat emptor	nunc pro tunc
de facto	per curiam
de jure	pro forma
estoppel	proximate cause
ex parte	quantum meruit
in rem	res judicata

§ 10.05 TWO MISUSED WORDS

Two misused words deserve special mention.

§ 10.05(a) Pleading

This word receives my vote as the most misused word in lawsuits. Attorneys frequently have a file folder they call "Pleadings." In courtroom corridors you often hear attorneys refer to their motion papers as "pleadings." Unfortunately, even the judges have succumbed.

This is a word of art, with a very specific meaning as defined in the rules. FRCP 7(a). The word also has considerable substantive meaning. A pleading, generally, consists of the affirmative statement of one's claim or the responsive statement by the opposing party. The typical affirmative pleading by a plaintiff is the complaint. By a defendant it is a counterclaim if against a plaintiff, a cross-claim if against another defendant, or a third-party complaint if against a new party brought in by the defendant. The responsive pleading is called an answer, except that with respect to a counterclaim it is called a reply.

The pleadings frame the scope of the action and, unless amended, frame the scope of the matters to be litigated. The only exceptions in terms of framing issues might be a pretrial order, which may supercede the pleadings, or an issue tried with the consent of all parties. FRCP 16, 15(b). Otherwise, the pleadings determine the contours of the action.

If other documents are not "pleadings," then what should we call them? The federal rules call them "motions and other papers," FRCP 7(b), and they may simply be referred to as "papers," "legal papers" or "documents."

§ 10.05(b) Cause Or Within Cause

Frequently lawyers refer in legal papers to the "cause" or the "within cause." I don't know what a "cause" is. The legal theory of the party may be a cause of action. However, the lawsuit itself is not a "cause." The federal rules at the outset state that there shall be one form of action, known as a "civil action." FRCP 2. Therefore, a lawsuit is an "action." It is not a cause.

§ 10.06 CONCLUSION

This manual is only a blueprint. You must build the structure. There is no substitute for actual practice. Start perhaps by critiquing (for yourself) papers drafted by others. Begin your own new style with something easy, such as captions, introductory clauses, or a proof of service. With desire and patience, your style will, in time, become plain and accurate English.

Table of Statutes, Rules, and Regulations

(References are to section numbers)

Federal Rules of Civil Procedure

Federal Rules of Civil Procedure — Forms

Index of Subjects

(References are to section numbers)